To Jaquar —

Dancing with Life

꧁ꕤ꧂

A Young Woman's Quest
for Art, Love, and Freedom

A Travel Memoir by
Dhyanis Carniglia

*Thanks for doing
your fine work!
with Admiration, Dhyanis*

Dancing with Life
A Young Woman's Quest
for Art, Love, and Freedom

A Travel Memoir by Dhyanis Carniglia

©2021 by Dhyanis Carniglia

United States of America

ISBN: 978-1-7364806-0-1

First Edition

Cover Art by Dhyanis Carniglia

Dedication

For Serena, my ephemeral traveler

Acknowledgments

With appreciation for the support and guidance
of those who encouraged this writing. First
to my husband who cheerfully greeted the
emergence of my inner author without
reading a word, and to his Mom Gini — my
dream mother-in-law — whose generous
gifts gave me the kickstart to do the work.

To those VIP along my journey, including my
first belly dance teacher Charlsa Knobloch,
Artur Rebelo and Ni (Ilda) Macia whose hearts
opened to me in Portugal and beyond, "Aunt
Rocky" (C. Varga Dinicu) who shared her vast
knowledge of Middle Eastern cultlures and
dance, and all those who have danced with me
as students or colleagues across the globe.

And to Aurora Winter for helping me shape
the raw material, Heidi Smith for her intuitive
coaching, Barbara Sedassy and Dorothea
O'Regan for their precious friendship and
shared adventures, my entire colorful family,
and of course the Benevolent Universe.

Contents

Preface

This memoir covers merely the highlights of my first forty years "growing up," or, now that it is written, my "youth." Baby Boomers were famous for staunchly not trusting anyone over thirty and then going into denial when we reached that ripe old age. We never wanted our decisions to be based on some dried-up old mores or the hypocrisy we saw everywhere. "Freedom" was the anthem and central guiding principle, so I, like so many others in the sixties and seventies, became a Bourgeois Bohemian with an adventurous prolonged youth.

I was raised to be a proper young lady, groomed for higher education and some sort of career. But alongside these expectations, our family was exuberantly outdoorsy and continually modeled rugged individualism. In the fifties, conservatism and fierce self-determination formed the Republican idea which swept the nation. It is not surprising so many of us Baby Boomers dove off into the promised autonomy of the counterculture. This is the best rationale I can offer for my own fierce self-determination — the volatile mixture of my insular (controlling) family and the attractive new whiff of freedom just as I approached adulthood.

In 1966, at 19 (and-a-half!), I tried to do the right thing by marrying instead of shacking up. Overnight I found myself in a life-threatening nightmare from which I eventually had to flee, with a toddler, into the wild zeitgeist of the late sixties and a whole new world to explore.

It was my plan to wait until I "could no longer dance" to relate these adventures. But since I find myself still dancing and working in a variety of artistic fields at age 73, that time may never come. I could die dancing! At a February 2020 Reboot Your Life Retreat in San Miguel de Allende, Mexico, I found myself telling bits of stories to the attendees and thinking these disparate tales should really all be in one place. When the retreat leader, Aurora Winter, presented us with an optional Write Your Book package, I felt that lightning bolt of providence. Bursting into tears I made the commitment then and there. Additionally the 2020 pandemic shut down all outside work and kept us indoors, giving me the enforced gift of time.

Reviewing one's life is revelatory, and not always comfortable. It so often appears that I was drifting along, influenced by the random people I met, and furthering my education with a haphazard syllabus. However at the time, it felt as if all the serendipity and connections led me to exactly the right experiences, always with angels protecting me through the most hazardous and harrowing bits. I was juggling the responsibilities of a young single mother, the unstructured freedom of the times, and my own natural industriousness and artistic potential. Throw into the mix a good measure of hot young Italian blood and come along for the ride.

It is my hope that my story might inspire or encourage readers on their own quests to follow their passions, true callings and true loves.

Mother Lion

"The difficulties of life are intended to make us better, not bitter." Anonymous

I made my own wedding dress, helped my cousin sew her maid of honor dress, and created a "traveling suit" to leave the rather somber reception at my parents' home. I was optimistic with every stitch, and my dreams were carefully sewn into those traditional garments. Those dreams were jarringly dashed when we reached our new apartment for the wedding night.

I don't know what triggered him, but Jim suddenly came at me like an enraged animal. I instinctively ran (naturally athletic and nimble as I was). I hid in the apartment laundry room, squeezed into the small crevice between the washing machine and wall. When he opened the door to look for me, I held my breath, hoping he would not hear my thumping heart. Somehow I escaped detection and spent the rest of the night huddled there, considering my big mistake. But too late. I could not admit my foolishness after insisting on this wedding. I had jumped out of the proverbial frying pan (a restrictive family), into a violent, unexpected fire! I had literally made my bed and pridefully felt I had to lie in it.

So I decided to stay and make the best of it. I weathered that volatile marriage for two years. There was abundant passion and laughter at one extreme, but the dominant theme was "us against them." It all revolved around my husband's wartime experience, leaving him with nightmares and the story that he was trained in the special services. As a wounded Navy Seal, Jim claimed that he had left the service and married without "their" permission and "they" would do nefarious things to split us up. One of these was to drug him, control him to attack me, and induce me to leave. But, *oh no!* In Chinese Astrology I was born in the Year of the Pig, very loyal and even more stubborn. I endured these recurring violent episodes, followed by profuse apologies, pronouncements of love, and yes, make-up sex.

Coming from such an insular family, I had no knowledge that this could be a typical pattern of instability or abuse and chose to believe his excuses. I sustained injuries including a broken nose (requiring a hospital visit where I refused to press charges), and a fist-induced miscarriage of that first pregnancy. He had called me at a menial job to come home immediately, using his "trance voice" to say "Your husband needs you." When I arrived, concerned, he simply stood me up against a wall and out of nowhere started punching my abdomen, over and over, until large clots of blood and fetus drained from my body, accompanied by severe cramping. At the hospital for a D&C, I let the doctor think it had occurred naturally.

We had moved from working class San Leandro to the more artsy and political environment of Berkeley in 1967. A student friend took us to a demonstration on the steps of Sproul Hall at the University of California so we could listen to the Students for a Democratic Society (SDS) and glimpse the unrest. SDS students at Kent State had recently been killed for demonstrating.

Our life however was one of simple survival. Finally Jim found a steady job in Berkeley. For extra cash I took in alterations, taught a basic painting class to a group of women assembled by my mother, and painted, while also attending a few classes at the prestigious California College of Arts and Crafts. I knew in my heart that I was an artist and really had no idea what style or message or medium to develop. But my dream was not to be completely derailed by this marriage.

We listened over and over to the new Beatles' album, *Sergeant Pepper's Lonely Hearts Club Band,* and played chess, which Jim had perfected to prove to himself how smart he was. My second pregnancy resulted in a healthy baby girl, Serena. My mother came to the hospital during my difficult labor to rub my feet and reassure me. I tried for a natural birth, but at the last minute the doctor used forceps to finish pulling her out of my small, unyielding body. All memory of the pain was immediately surpassed by the blissful high of holding a newborn, miraculous bundle of precious life. All reports of such feelings cannot approach the reality of that divine joy. My sister gave me a congratulatory card in which she had copied the section "On Children" from *The Prophet* by Kahlil Gibran, which begins:

> *"Your children are not your children. They are the sons and daughters of Life's longing for itself. They come through you but not from you, and though they are with you, yet they belong not to you."*

The significance of that poem for me was only revealed some years later. I was fortunate that breast feeding had at that time renewed popularity. Sometimes I kept Serena cuddled next to me after nursing at night, against the common "wisdom," because the bond felt so strong I could not bear to return her to her crib.

For a time we were happy, but soon Jim's "nightmares" returned, both sleeping and waking. I got nervous enough to tell a couple of neighbors to check on me if they heard yelling from our apartment. One of them drove me to a hospital appointment with a resident psychologist to whom I poured out the story. He concluded that I was in a dangerous situation with a potential paranoid schizophrenic, but there was nothing he could do. His advice was either to leave or call the police to witness the next scene of domestic violence.

The very next time the trance-like nocturnal third person began (according to Jim, a voice of someone from the CIA speaking through him), he said, "Mrs. H, if you refuse again to do our bidding, you may find your baby strangled in her crib." This horrifying image jolted me into finally taking action, if not for myself, then for my child. That is when I revealed all to my family, who were quick to the rescue.

On that Berkeley morning of 1968, I quietly waited for my husband to leave for work, then called my father at his insurance company in San Francisco. He listened to my confession of the abuse I had endured, and covered up, for the entire two years of this ill-advised marriage. Within hours he had me loading our belongings, including one-year-old Serena's crib, into a rented anonymous truck. He met us at a safe distance and escorted us to a motel in another county to shield us from any consequences.

I had left a note for Jim, saying that I would talk to him only after he sought professional help. Instead he sought out my sensitive and gullible younger brother Pete at his high school and had him in tears with convincing histrionics and pleas of undying love for me. Of course my brother revealed our sanctuary and soon my parents shipped us off to L.A. to stay with a sympathetic aunt and uncle, where we could recuperate in peaceful surroundings.

What a change from constantly being on edge and waiting for the next explosive episode. I played with and tended to little Serena without fear. My aunt was a very calm social worker, good listener, and wise advisor. While safe-harboring there I painted a tall impressionistic floral arrangement for her entry hall — and wondered what I would do next.

Child of the Fifties

"The era we are living in today is a dream of coming true."
Walt Disney

My parents fell in love before The War (WWII) but waited to marry until my father returned from overseas. Barbara, or "Babs," the dark-haired independent Italian beauty who would become mother of three had a wartime office job at Pan Am (Pan American Airlines). Richard, or "Dick," the light, wavy-haired handsome blue-eyed (half Italian) man she was determined to marry was sent to a desk job in a tent in Australia. He did not qualify for active duty due to the loss of one eye as a child from an infection from a rusty nail. No one could tell: the glass eye matched his good blue eye so perfectly, although the pupil did not dilate with different light.

For their wedding in 1946 one of my mother's cousins, who had married a real estate mogul, gifted them with a prime vacant lot in the Oakland, California, hills. I arrived on Valentine's Day 1947, two weeks late, apparently waiting for the special day of love to make an entrance.

My father, following in the footsteps of his own insurance "career man" father, had a lower echelon white collar job as an underwriter at Fireman's Fund Insurance Company, then located in San Francisco. He finished his college degree that had been interrupted by the war. My mother was committed to being a proper housewife with emphasis on creating a strong family life. She had been an orphaned immigrant at the age of ten, speaking very little English, and farmed out to a "mean stepmother" of an aunt. She was treated precisely as a personal house slave, a classic 1930s San Francisco version of the Cinderella story.

Apparently I resemble my maternal grandmother Anita, both in her appearance and possibly in her propensity for adventure. Born in 1890, she became a stenographer who worked closely with A.P. Giannini, the man who helped rebuild San Francisco after the devastating 1906 earthquake. He founded the Bank of Italy and loaned money at low interest to the many whose businesses were destroyed in the fires, later to expand and become the Bank of America. While working there she met a dashing Italian man who whisked her off to Brazil where he had a high-ranking position at the American Consulate. This was his second marriage and no one was ever quite sure he had legally terminated his first.

It was during the 1920s high life of beautiful clothing, jewelry and parties, though Anita somehow managed to give birth to three daughters (my mother's twin died at birth). The two surviving girls were raised by a German nanny, Portuguese servants, and the nuns at boarding school; and they rarely saw their parents.

When my mother turned eight, her father cast them out to a smaller house and eventually onto a ship heading for New York. They took a train with a sleeping compartment across the country to her mother's family of origin in Oakland, California. Within the year, my grandmother died of pneumonia or perhaps a broken heart after betrayal by her husband (this refutes my cousins' theory that I am like her). Surviving all this, my mother was determined to become a model American wife, create a "normal" family, and give her own children all the best opportunities.

For my first two years of life, we lived in a walk-up apartment in the city. My few memories include laundry hanging inside to dry over the radiators and the elderly lady next door allowing me to play with her dazzling array of colored knitting needles on the floor like pick-up sticks. When my parents had saved enough funds for house construction to begin on the vacant lot, I was curious about every detail from framing to painting (I still relish the fragrant smell of freshly sawn redwood beams). I was told stories later about how articulate and candid a two-year-old I was, following the workmen, asking questions, and not the least bit self-conscious or shy.

It has thus remained a mystery to me what happened to change that confident little person into the scared and self-critical girl I clearly remember being when it was time for kindergarten. For days I cried and clung to my mother, begging her not to leave me at the school gate. It took so much courage to pass through the upper grades' raucous schoolyard to get to my classroom. Once we had settled into the modest but nice three-bedroom house with hardwood floors, a living room fireplace, and a great all-around backyard, my first sibling soon arrived.

At three-and-a-half I must have felt dethroned by baby Louise, known then as "Sissy." She soon blossomed into the cutest blue-eyed, curly blond angelic twinkly toddler ever. Next to her I was the serious dark and brooding type. At a family wedding of a distant cousin we rarely saw, a highly groomed woman in a long fur coat and blonde pageboy (a ringer for the glamorous Grace Kelly) approached us and exclaimed to my mother about Sissy, "Oh Barbara, I have never seen such a beautiful child!" Barely glancing at me she added, "This one is nice too, but..." and continued rhapsodizing over my little sister.

I started comparing myself to everyone else in every detail, finding flaws like my calves were too skinny, my nose too big, hair too straight, and I did not get to take ballet. Little brother Peter came along in 1952 when I was five-and-a-half but did not stoke any sibling rivalry. I remember only being fascinated when, during one diaper change, he peed straight up into the air like a fountain. Boys were such alien creatures. As he grew, I thought he looked adorable in his short pants outfits, and he was easier to boss around. My sister and I would put dresses on him and call him "Sally" when we played "family."

I could almost taste colors. My favorite "toy" of all was a brand new box of 64 crayons, and my favorite subject was fashion. I cut out my own paper dolls and traced their silhouettes to create endless colored wardrobes. My system was to pick one color at a time to combine with every other color, one dress at a time, then on down the rows of colors, first in pairs, then in trios. Each color combination produced its own unique feeling, vibration, "taste." These early impressions still resonate with me today! When we were given an Audubon bird coloring book, I spent hours trying to reproduce the look of iridescence I saw on hummingbirds, mallard ducks, blackbirds and starlings, first with crayons, then with watercolors. It seemed I was born to see the world as an artist. Anything that sparkled gave me inexplicable joy, from the morning dew to the glitter-covered crepe paper "hula skirt" my friend gave me as a party favor.

Mom was quite the seamstress, often making clothes for us girls and herself. When the "padded" circle skirts became popular (think fifties poodle skirts made of quilted fabric), she got out the portable Singer sewing machine. I insisted on mine being lavender and turquoise or, I pouted, I would go without. Difficult indeed, since ultimatums from kids were not usually honored, plus that was an unusual color combination for the time. Probably because she was also artistic and quite particular about her own clothing, my mother searched until she found lavender quilted fabric printed all over with small turquoise flowers. I felt so lovely in that skirt; with a white sleeveless blouse and white sandals, it was my favorite unforgettable outfit in second grade.

Our mother did everything to be the Ideal Mom, while keeping expenses down. Each morning when Dad left for work, she sweetly placed a small pink rose (from her Cecil Brunner bush) in his lapel. She helped us plant a basic vegetable garden and showed us how to tend it and delight in picking what we grew.

Her cooking was wonderful, including her use of organ meats in the Italian way she had learned from her aunts. She served a rice dish with lamb kidneys which even my pickiest cousin would eat when she was told we were having "lamb." In rotation on the family menu were also lamb's tongue with pasta, beef hearts, and of course beef and chicken liver. Early on Mom found the health food guru Adele Davis so we were served "tiger's milk" (unappetizing brewer's yeast and molasses in milk), wheat germ, brown bread and avocado sandwiches, all making our school lunches a constant embarrassment. In summertime we had homemade "popsicles" from lemonade and were not allowed Coca Cola.

But we did enjoy great baked goods, especially for family parties. Counting us, there were nineteen cousins plus several generations of adults from both sides of the Italian family trees. Mom was such an enthusiastic hostess for holidays and birthday celebrations, making each one special. Elderly maiden "Great Aunt Mary," who had been a dressmaker and taught me the strength of "backstitching" by hand, had her birthday in spring. The table was set with daffodils from the garden on the crocheted lace tablecloth Aunt Mary had made with her own hands and given as a wedding present. Mom baked our aunt's favorite orange zest cake, drizzled with tangy lemon glaze. I can still see the pleased look on Aunt Mary's face and taste a vestige of that cake when the daffodils bloom.

Mom was also one of my Brownie and Girl Scout Troop parent leaders, helping us accumulate badges and driving us to activities. She always included our three closest cousins on outings like Christmas shopping expeditions to the holiday faire in Sausalito or trips to museums. She helped us host overnights and small parties for our friends. Later I came to resent this constant "supervision" but now acknowledge how much gusto she put into parenting.

Dad gave us entertainment in the form of elaborate stories he would spin by the fireplace, creating suspenseful serials. When we would try to guess an outcome, he would suppress a smile and ask "Who's telling this story?" and sometimes incorporate our ideas into the next chapter so we could exclaim "I knew it!"

Throughout grammar school my best friend Beanie lived a few houses away, so we walked to the bus stop together every day. After school we got into building forts and hacking trails through the underbrush on the hillside below our house. When her family got a TV (before we were allowed to), I would visit her basement to idolize Annette Funicello on the *Mickey Mouse Club*, and later dance along to *American Bandstand*. Our grammar school neighborhood was so WASP that the handful of Catholic kids, of which I was one, provided the "diversity." We were considered different because we were taken out of class every week to study our catechism with the nuns in a makeshift classroom in a garage across the street to prepare for First Communion and then Confirmation.

First Travels on the
Daylight Train 1947.
Mom, Dad, Me

Siblings 1952. Louise (Sissy), D, Peter

First Communion 1954. With Cousins Jen,
Kathleen, D, Louise, Roberta

Proud Mom 1957. Louise, Mom, D, Peter

Redwood Bowmen Archery Range,
Oakland, 1958. Peter, D, Louise

Montana Trailer Camping 1959. Dhyanis, Peter

Swinging Sixties

"For the times, they are a changin'." Bob Dylan

For our first year of middle school, we were bussed down to the "flats" of Oakland to a very integrated school. At first I was intimidated by the stampede of tall athletic black kids crowding the halls of this scary junior high, but I found that at the after-school dances on Fridays they were my best teachers. It was the infancy of rock n' roll, so we heard the music of Chubby Checker, Fats Domino, and the pounding piano of Little Richard, mixed in with scandalous "Elvis the Pelvis," really for the first time.

The radio at home played a steady stream of Dinah Shore, Frank Sinatra, Doris Day, Bing Crosby, Gogi Grant (The Wayward Wind), all of whose hits I memorized and still enjoy singing. But this new bee-bop was modern and belonged to our generation. Historically this was the first time there was peace and economic security enough for the kids to develop their own culture. As yet we were not bothered by knowledge of the Cold War and the threat of atomic annihilation. It was the "I Like Ike" Eisenhower era and we (kids) felt safe and sheltered in spite of occasional school air-raid drills.

I really pined for dance classes, but Dad played the accordion and harmonica and our parents agreed that we should learn to read music. A small upright Baldwin Spinet piano was purchased for the house and a classical teacher selected. This strict man (father of one of my sister's classmates) required us to also take a weekly music theory class with his handsome young assistant. A crush was born and I worked hard to impress "Mr. Gary." He rewarded me by informing me that I have perfect pitch since at that time I could identify random notes he picked out on the piano. In seventh grade choir class I got the enviable solo part in the holiday program to sing "and a partridge in a pear tree."

We attended musical theater productions at the nearby outdoor amphitheater in the Oakland hills, and I was convinced I could do the lead role of Laurey in *Oklahoma*, no problem. Mom could type, so she helped me prepare a script of a couple of scenes and songs with carbon copies to pass out to a few choir classmates. When the day came to present this to the class, the boy I "liked" did not want to perform the male lead. His replacement was more of a class clown and I made sure everyone knew I did not intend the romantic lyrics for him personally. Needless to say, the faces I made as "asides" completely undermined the performance, even if I did sing on key.

There were also stressful piano recitals in front of judges. Somehow those experiences in front of people did not did not alleviate my acute shyness. In spite of practicing to become the next Debbie Reynolds (singing "Tammy" day and night in front of a mirror) I remained in agony and at a loss with strangers, though a star in my daydreams.

Our family was solidly middle class (upwardly mobile as my father was promoted), but everything was "do it yourself." It seemed anything a family could do together we did. There was an archery range in the regional park and all five of us were fitted with bows of just the right size, weight and "draw." My father had a workshop room adjoining the carport where he made our arrows. We all became adept at hitting the centers of the targets on hay bales along the trails. Memorably, once on the range, my father stepped in a yellow jacket nest and the mad hornets swarmed up his pant legs. Must have been some painful stings — without understanding the full implications, I felt so sorry for him I cried.

One year I got a simple Brownie camera for Christmas and Dad set up a darkroom. He taught us how to mix the trays of chemicals and time each step to develop our own black and white film. I took a lot of artsy photos in the Sierra snow. My cousin and I took pensive portraits of each other and developed them, superimposed in a creative double exposure. Mom later did a lot of photography for art shows.

We started camping and fishing when little brother Peter was two and I was seven. The first time, at the ominously named Snag Lake, I was just cold, miserable and wondering what was fun about this. But soon I was helping pound in tent stakes and learning to cook pancakes on a griddle over the fire. Dad had various handguns and a .22 caliber rifle for which he made his own molten-lead bullets. We all learned to shoot at tin cans on fences, and I remember my mother leaning out the living room window aiming that gun at gophers that kept digging up the back garden.

One place we set up camp for a couple of weeks each summer was called Sand Flat on the Stanislaus River. Another family of regulars there invited us to their nightly campfire for toasted marshmallows and sing-alongs, with Dad on the harmonica. As usual, seeing the world with an artist's eye, I brought along a watercolor set and tried diligently to capture images of the riverbed stones through the flowing water, as well as the wind in the tall pines, never to my complete satisfaction.

Our parents kept us busy with family projects. They had us picking grapes at a Sonoma vineyard for winemaking.

Dad made beer and delicious root beer (with occasional exploded bottles), and of course we cranked out our own rich ice cream for special occasions. We dug for small seasonal cockles in nearby Tomales Bay. We took three-week vacation-work trips to different areas of the United States, pulling a rented seventeen-foot trailer (harbinger of RV living), staying at campsites and trailer parks as we explored the countryside and monuments.

Dad was sent by his company to branch offices in other cities to attend meetings and solve problems, and we were glad to accompany him. We traversed the Southwest and Native American cultures when he was assigned to Albuquerque, New Mexico. Other years we visited The Great Salt Lake area, the Rockies, Yellowstone National Park (Old Faithful Geyser), and the Snake River in Idaho (fresh frog legs). I took loads of photos with that little Brownie camera and still have them in scrapbooks.

We three children thought our life was normal, if not a tetch overly family-centric. In retrospect we had a rich childhood with more opportunities than most to experience the world and nurture our specific talents. But by high school I was "chafing at the bit" between feeling restricted by the emphasis on getting the grades required to qualify for the University of California (a family expectation) and the struggle to navigate the social hierarchies at school. It seemed that everyone else's parents were more lenient, and I had little chance to experiment in social situations outside the family fold.

The world was moving on. Sonny and Cher had shown us a more sophisticated singing couple (honorable mention for the Bob Mackie beaded gowns she wore every week) and the long-haired Beatles had made their appearance on the previously milk-toast Ed Sullivan Show. They had every girl swooning and picking her favorite (George, the "deep" one for me). One of my friends had begun to sing folk songs, accompanying herself on the guitar, and I followed suit, emulating Peter, Paul and Mary and Joan Baez. And we were shocked into more political awareness when, in 1963, our beloved President Kennedy was assassinated in plain sight.

Every day I got off the bus and headed for the bathroom mirror to "rat" my hair, apply black eyeliner, powder pink Julie Christie lipstick, and roll up my skirt at the waist. This was a vain attempt to fit in with the "popular girls," though one of them told me, "You're cute but you don't have the personality." Exactly — how did you get "personality" if you were stuck with your family all the time, every weekend either at the cabin, or now on the family sailboat.

My mother had gotten the sailing bug by taking classes in eight-foot El Toros on Lake Merritt in Oakland, then encouraged the rest of us to take the class as well. After capsizing a few times into the brown-green mucky lake water I was not that interested, but Dad was captivated and became a boat owner. Although Mom turned out great meals from the small galley, I came along only for the sun bathing. Escaping into Ayn Rand's The Fountainhead, stretched out on the prow in a bikini, I imagined my name was "Dominique."

Later the family moved from Oakland to San Rafael, Marin County, by the bay to moor the boat on the canal in the backyard. My brother Pete became an avid sailor and finds great solace in wind and waves. He was also super-talented, building from scratch his first vehicle in high school, a "dune buggy" to race on the sand, and he went off to college to study film-making.

The best thing about high school was that it offered great electives. I was finally able to take the coveted dance classes for PE, listed as Modern Dance. However when the film Westside Story was released, our teacher created a jazz routine to the song "Cool" and even I felt cool doing it. I also took a commercial art class in which the students created posters for school activities, and all the fancy lettering I had been developing by writing boy's names on my blank book covers paid off. And, with apparent indefatigable energy, I opted to join a night tailoring class at another high school, taught by an Eastern European woman with expert precision sewing skills. I made the most unusually glamorous, Greek-Goddess-inspired, white crepe prom dress.

New Year at Dorrington 1963. Mom, Dad

Jamming at Dorrington 1963. Dad on harmonica
with D, Louise

Supplies for Dorrington Weekend 1964. Dhyanis

Chico and Dhyanis at Galt Round-Up 1964

Fancy Home Photography 1964. Cousin Kathleen, D

Senior Prom Sophisticate 1964

Studying the Good Life at
UCSB 1965

On Religion

"Miracles happened. Virgin birth...made perfect sense. There was a Holy Ghost. Guardian angels walked beside us and our patron saints really did put in a good word for us every now and then." John William Tuohy

Dad's family was apparently agnostic, with no church affiliation at all. My mother had been sent to Catholic school by her austere aunt and had married in the church. She decided to raise us as Roman Catholics to impart some sort of moral guidance. We were taken to church every Sunday and progressed through the sacraments, along with our three closest girl cousins.

During the 1950s, hats were required in church, so everyone was truly in their Sunday Best. The kids took communion first, then watched from the front pews as the adults filed up to the altar. My post-communion amusement was picking out and combining my favorite hat, rhinestone broach, dress, shoes, etc., to create in my mind that week's winning outfit. After all, the Mass was said in Latin and the sermon was usually a boring, guilt-inducing rendition of "God is watching you every second," and singing was reserved for the rare holiday. A girl had to have *some* fun.

We were taught that only we Catholics who confessed our sins could ever make it into heaven. Seven is said to be "the age of reason" and right about then I reasoned that this could not be true. Being in such a minority, what would then happen to all the Protestant and Jewish kids I knew at public school? And why was it stressed as such a sin to attend other religious services? When I went to a sleepover at the home of one of the nicest girls, the family took me to their Presbyterian church on Sunday morning. I was so curious I risked the great transgression, knowing I could confess it and be absolved.

All I could glean from their service was a similar belief in God and Jesus, but with a notable lack of the more sumptuous theatrical trappings of Catholicism. I knew for sure this wonderful girl and her super-nice Mom did not deserve to go to hell. If this dogma of the church was irreconcilable, then what else might be?

My favorite cousin went to college a couple years ahead of me and discovered Baha'i Meetings on campus at U.C. Berkeley and invited me, still in high school. This originally Persian Faith (established in 1863) teaches the essential worth of all religions and unity of all people. Here was a religion that made sense and these meetings were mind-expanding. I appreciated the basic tenets of World Peace, need for universal education, and especially equality of all — women and men, rich and poor, all races, religions, etc.

In the end it was the struggle with hormones that finally led me to reject Catholicism as The Truth. I pretty much had to choose between it and sex. One Sunday during my sophomore year of college I went to the Goleta Chapel near the U.C. Santa Barbara campus to say my farewell. My search for "Mr. Right" was not, however, guided by great judgment of character.

My Daughter's Father

"It's what you learn after you know it all that counts."
John Wooden

After two years living in the dorm at U.C. Santa Barbara and adding all the available art classes to the required liberal arts curriculum, I found art to be the only classes that truly "turned me on." I intended to transfer to U.C. Berkeley, switch majors from English to art, with hopes of moving into a shared apartment off campus.

Home for the summer, I got involved in a shoplifting fiasco with a bad boy ex, which I did not care to confess to my parents (detailed in the subsequent chapter "Flashback City"). I needed a summer job urgently to cover the costs of a lawyer to help me take care of this matter. I was told that as a first-time-offender it could be expunged from the record, but this would incur fees. I joined a temp agency which placed me in several offices and finally in a Bank of America administrative office in downtown San Francisco doing routine filing and typing.

An old flame from high school sought me out — Jim, who had amused me in our homeroom class period before being expelled from our junior year for smoking in the bathroom. He claimed he had nobly grabbed the cigarette from his adopted brother to take the rap for him. His mother had signed him into the Navy where he had spent the last three years, and he was back home to visit her. She had received a letter saying he was AWOL (absent without leave), but he had a different story. I have a vivid memory of us walking the back trails of the Oakland hills, him pinning me to a tree, telling me how fabulous I was, and thinking this could be love. I confided to him all about the shoplifting charge and how and where I was working to clear it.

One day at the bank I was called in by management and fired for "concealing an arrest." Jim took this opportunity to convince me to hitchhike to Yosemite National Park and camp out with him. It was not until much later I connected those two events — it was he who had called the bank, impersonating the authorities, to get me fired, nearly unemployable, and free to go with him on an adventure. We scrounged a double sleeping bag, an iron skillet, a sack of potatoes, and he initiated me to the ways of the road.

I admired his easy charm with the people who picked us up, waitresses, park rangers, neighboring campers — everyone! I still harbored a good measure of residual shyness and hoped his ease with people would rub off on me. One night I felt a bear's claws pick up my foot, then gently put it down — not food! When I told Jim, he picked up the iron skillet and hustled us both to the top of a nearby boulder, but I had not been frightened.

In Yosemite Jim began to have violent nightmares reliving his military experiences. He clung to me, almost begging me to marry him. With true naivete I agreed, thinking that I alone could help him through and banish the nightmares. He began telling me of his special assignment in Cypress as coxswain of a small boat delivering medical supplies and arms to both sides — to help fuel a skirmish between Greeks and Turks (to what end I still do not comprehend, but would not put it past NATO or other organizations). It was on one of these missions that his boat was hit by mortar fire and most of his best buddies were blown to pieces. He survived by jumping into the water and assuming fetal position as the blast sprayed shrapnel with such force it caused him to literally bleed from every pore. The term PTSD had yet to be coined in those days, and I imagined that his feeling loved by me would cure any residual effects of these horrific war experiences.

Jim told his mother he had enrolled in a real estate course, which he soon abandoned, preferring to spend his time seducing me. She came home early one evening when he was supposed to be in class, finding us together. She threw us out of her house, aiming my boots at me and yelling "whore!" She was not that pleased to learn of our engagement. My parents were completely devastated by my insistence on this commitment to "throw away my education and marry this person from the wrong side of the tracks." Jim had no high school diploma, little ambition and zero prospects.

But I stubbornly held to my promise to him while my family dutifully arranged a traditional white wedding at the Catholic church of my youth. In preparation, the priest asked us to sign an oath not to use any means of birth control. I inconveniently had my period on the wedding day, but that was the last one. Mom later said she had believed I only insisted on getting married because I was already pregnant, though it had not technically been the case. I wanted to be free of parental control, plus I believed this was an epic love. At nineteen-and-a-half I felt like such an adult, marrying this intrinsically clever guy who had seen the world. He had tantalized me with tales of Naples and the Blue Grotto of Capri and all his dramatic experiences in the Navy.

By then I had heard all the details of his traumatic rescue from the island and his recovery at the Philadelphia Naval Hospital, where he claimed "they" had done tests on his brain, using him as a guinea pig for LSD experiments. Instead of discharging him, they sent the letter saying he was AWOL to his mother but kept him as an undercover agent to help break up drug rings in the Philly area. He had been "programmed" to infiltrate as a pool shark and intercept drug trafficking. I have never known if Jim read this in a novel, simply could not admit mediocrity and invented this tale, or if there was a shred of truth to any of this fantastical plot, but he had me convinced. This story was our marriage secret, ironically holding us together. As a young wife, I did not want to break his trust, and so I stayed until he threatened our baby daughter.

After the time spent incommunicado, safely out of danger with my Southern California relatives, I returned to the Bay Area. The landlady in Berkeley complained that Jim had disappeared, leaving the apartment battered and empty. My very capable brother volunteered to rent a floor sander to repair some mysterious deep grooves in the hardwood floor, and we found some used syringes in the corners. I really did not know whether Jim had been influenced by drugs the whole of our marriage, or whether he resorted to them afterwards, but certainly some of his erratic behavior might be attributed to them.

Other thoughts were that combined with PTSD, the responsibility of having a wife and then a child was just too much, especially since he no doubt felt inferior to my family's standard for me. I had certainly discovered in myself a huge capacity for instability, passion, pleasure, and pain, and had learned something of my strength and how to survive life's hard knocks.

Hip Ad Agency and Patrick

"Don't wait for your ship to come in. Row out to meet it."
Unknown

Newly divorced in 1968, temp-typing in San Francisco, one ad agency kept me on permanently. Jack Wodell Associates specialized in film publicity. I began as a receptionist and thought I might end up in the art department, but I was moved instead to secretary for the three account execs. I dressed smartly and strode through the city in tall high-heeled boots and "mod" mini-skirts. I hired in-house babysitters to watch Serena by day. When actors came to town to promote a film, I was sometimes sent to their hotel to answer phones and run errands. For my small contribution to his 1969 film tour for *The Magus*, Anthony Quinn rewarded me with a quick hearty kiss (which I now might classify as "consensual").

Our most "hip" ad exec was working with the young film-makers George Lucas and Francis Ford Coppola on their first public effort *THX1138*, and when they were audition-ing for their next script, I went. The role included a nude scene, so they had me prance around au natural. I was completely comfortable with my strong and graceful young body, but they hired someone with more experience, as I had no resume or acting chops, unless you counted the crash course of "improv" acting I had learned to implement during my dramatic marriage.

The agency hosted the Annual San Francisco Film Festival and for a couple of weeks I reported to work in the press room issuing badges and media kits to critics and film luminaries. I became fascinated by an eccentric French writer and film critic, outfitted in green army fatigues with all the pockets bulging with notebooks, cigars and brandy flask. He had playful brown eyes flashing from a deeply etched, chiseled face, reminiscent of a wise "chief." As if to emphasize the likeness, he wore Native American jewelry and a woven headband. He had renounced France and resided in Quebec but had been in California for three years, writing and immersing himself in our youth culture, our music, and our revolutionary potential.

He was a self-proclaimed "Marxist-Leninist-Maoist," and in one pocket always carried Mao Tse-tung's "Little Red Book" (and gifted me a copy). He was a champion of all oppressed peoples and adopted the sacred numbers of many North American tribes, based on the four directions, which showed up in all his work.

Patrick (Pa-*treek*) was raised in France and as a young boy remembered hiding from passing German soldiers in a roadside ditch during the war. He adopted the nickname "Le Bison Ravi" (Delighted Buffalo) and named all his close friends in the same manner. I became "American Beauty of the Purple Sage," accompanying him into the world of art films, especially at the Berkeley Repertory Cinema. According to him, Jean-Luc Goddard was the most innovative, while Francois Truffaut, also of the French "New Wave," was "reactionary" or "petit-bourgeois," the most pejorative pronouncement. He loved (and resembled) Buster Keaton, physical comedian and actor-filmmaker of the silent film era, with his stoic deadpan reaction to all manner of catastrophe.

But never did we frequent the mainstream films for which I typed press releases every week at the agency. Patrick truly believed in the world-changing influence of the arts and that artists should not waste that opportunity by echoing the status quo. Mao's chapter on art proclaims that art is tied to class and has been used as propaganda by the ruling class; he states that ideally art should be allowed to flourish naturally among the proletariat. This did indeed make me question what possible contribution I could make in the artistic realm.

Patrick also believed that women should have a stronger voice and listened to me, especially during long talks in the bath. He was then thirty-six to my twenty-two (the year I knew everything!). He did not drive, but I took him on a cross-country road trip, with Serena, to show him the natural wonders and historic sites of America. We also visited Wolf House in Glen Ellen, Sonoma, the home of one of his literary idols, Jack London.

And on December 6, 1969, we attended the ill-fated Altamont Speedway free rock concert, organized by the headliner Rolling Stones to end their North American tour. This was billed as "Woodstock West" and people came from near and far to gather on the desolate hills of prickly dried grass and dirt clots for a full Saturday of music and camaraderie. The roads were packed by eleven a.m. when we, in our friends' car, arrived and parked along the highway a couple of miles from the site.

We trekked in and wedged ourselves into a space quite far from the stage, which was constructed at the bottom of the hill. Patrick started drinking beer (and whatever was in his flask) and I noticed that the portable restrooms were few and far away, and in any case unreachable through the dense crowd. It was reported that over 300,000 fans were in attendance and the sound system was sub-par. We heard a couple of bands, including Jefferson Airplane, and saw waves of disturbance ahead near the stage.

Apparently the Hell's Angels had been hired for security and were reacting violently to anyone who got near their bikes or tried to breach the stage. We heard Grace Slick appealing to the crowd to calm down: "This is supposed to be about *love*, people!" At one point Patrick embraced me fully on the ground and I felt his urine seeping into my clothing. It was a miserable event, and we learned that someone had been actually killed right there by the Hell's Angels. We packed up and left early, well before the "Stones" arrived, disappointed like everyone else by the sour vibes and violence, the antithesis of Woodstock.

Patrick was staying in the small back garden guesthouse of a French couple in Berkeley. My apartment and job were in "the city" (San Francisco). Whenever Serena visited her beloved grandparents, some weekends, I would hitchhike across the Bay Bridge to spend time with him in Berkeley where he held court with his multi-ethnic, politically engaged friends. One Friday, a compact and nice-looking African American named Ike, gave me a ride and offered me $20 an hour to "pose nude" at a Berkeley photo studio (with the shades pulled down over the windows for night shoots). I wanted the extra dollars for Christmas gifts (especially expensive bottles of liquors like Pernod for Patrick) and agreed. The photographer put on music and asked me to dance and, as I was doing so, Ike disrobed and joined me.

I went back a couple of times, but finally refused when dancing evolved into more than I had bargained for. I asked to see the pictures and found them highly esthetic with the contrasting skin tones of two beautiful people. Later Ike came to San Francisco to attempt to recruit me back, but I refused. He was quite understanding when he saw my young daughter in her crib through the door of the living room. I had not agreed to pornography in the first place and was probably naive to assume anything less. I never even told Patrick about it, or how I had been able to afford to shop at "City of Paris" for his exclusive imported gifts.

Montreal Migration

"Adversity is like a strong wind. It tears away from us all but the things that cannot be torn, so that we see ourselves as we really are." Arthur Golden

When, in the summer of 1970, Patrick was ready to return to Quebec, I offered to drive him, with the idea of moving there with him. We packed his belongings (contained in a wicker trunk full of books and mementos), Serena's, and mine, and prepared to leave the Bay Area indefinitely. My poor mother was in tears, saying good-bye to her grand-daughter and watching us drive away with this quirky Frenchman. When Patrick met her, he actually said, "If I weren't with the daughter I'd be with the mother," to which my mom retorted knowingly, "Flatterer." But I was under his Continental spell.

With everything strapped to the roof of my VW squareback, we made it to Thunder Bay, Ontario, when the overloaded engine simply died. A young mechanic offered to store our heavy items (shipping them later) and take the car in trade for that service. We continued by bus and knocked on the door of one of Patrick's old friends in the middle of the night. They welcomed us and though bilingual, spent the rest of the night catching up with Patrick in French. I had studied for a couple of years in high school but struggled to understand real conversations and languished on the floor, desperate for sleep.

We moved to a quaint cottage in the Gaspesie, 500 miles up the St. Lawrence River, with friends — two other writers, one with a wife and child. We got on well, taking long walks along the river gathering natural materials for art projects while Patrick wrote. It was a chilly October when a disturbing event dominated the radio news. The Deputy Premier of Quebec, Pierre LaPorte, was found dead in the trunk of a car owned by a known separatist and member of the FLQ (*Front de Libération du Québec*). A War Measures Act was invoked across Canada to quell the insurrection. Under this martial law, many artists with leftist leanings were arrested and detained for the next three weeks, including the popular singer Pauline Julien.

Armed police came to arrest the three men in our house because the former summer residents had been active members of the FLQ, though none of *us* had been involved. The other woman and I huddled fearfully by the radio for news, in ignorance of the fate of our men. After several tense days, the police knocked again, this time to take me and Serena to a detention center in Quebec City. They had tracked my passport to our entry point in Vancouver where I had been given only a two-week vacation visa (I planned to find a job and apply for residency). I was in violation by several months and was to be deported. Though technically guilty, I felt self-righteous about this interference in our innocent private lives.

The detention center held two other women with whom we talked in the common area by day. One was from Ghana who simply came to Canada with no visa. The other, from Portugal, cried continuously and spoke no English or French. She smiled through her tears when little Serena approached to tell her "everything would be alright." The matronly guards were sweet and brought in a cake for Serena's third birthday on October 23 to share with the other detainees.

Asking for an appeal, I was sent to Toronto to make my plea, based on love, to an immovable stern-faced panel. They contended that "If he loves you, he should marry you, and only then could you remain in Canada legally." However, Patrick was not yet divorced from his English-Canadian wife with two sons whom he had not seen for years. He claimed he wanted nothing to do with lawyers so would not bother with a legal divorce. As this ruled out marrying me, Serena and I were put on a plane and sent back to my parents in California, who were happy to see their granddaughter.

I spent many hours on the phone with Patrick and others, exploring ways to beat the system. We were determined not to let the authorities separate us for any reason! One idea was to marry a Swiss-Canadian friend now living in Sausalito, so we could swap nationalities. The fellow was willing, but his lawyer advised against it to prevent future complications. When Patrick finally gave in to calling his estranged wife to request a divorce, she laughed and laughed, revealing that she had divorced him three years ago on the grounds of desertion when he left for the U.S. Then, even more against his principles, Patrick appealed to the immigration authorities for an official pardon for me with the promise of marriage.

I flew to Champlain in upstate New York to await his escort across the border. I spent a week in a hotel frequented by transient truckers, babysitting the son of an itinerant singer/stripper while she entertained at the bar downstairs. An elderly local man who befriended us in the restaurant dealt in "carnival glass" and palmistry. When I asked him to read our palms, he said it was bad luck to read that of very young children, but I pressed him anyway. He took a quick look at Serena's hand, closed it, and announced to me, "You will have a lot of pain," saying no more. A day later during an afternoon nap, Serena had a seizure, which scared me to the core. A town doctor theorized that the seizure could have been caused by damage from forceps to a small part of her brain at birth. His prognosis was that she would outgrow it, but he prescribed phenobarbital and sent us on our way. I wondered if this was part of the fortune teller's prophecy.

In Montreal Patrick had rented a dingy apartment on Avenue de l'Esplanade, not far from Mont Royal Park, in a neighborhood mixed with Quebecoise working class, Greek, and Orthodox Jewish immigrants. Sprinkled among the blocks were basic Greek restaurants, mom & pop grocery stores, a fresh bagel factory, and of course taverns. There was a room for Serena and an office space for Patrick's writing. I brightened it up with paint and fabric.

We spent prolonged conversational soaks in the bathtub. He encouraged me to speak my truth on the topic of marriage, so I told him I would probably not be marrying him (or anyone) if not for the circumstances. At that time the Women's Liberation Movement was heating up and everything was seen through a new filter. Marriage was considered a patriarchal institution in which women were typically "colonized by men." A married woman took on the identity of her husband instead of autonomously following her own calling. Patrick was visibly deflated and although we wrote our poetic vows and married at a friend's cabin in a maple forest, the urgency of our love was lost. I learned the hard way that one need not spell out every thought.

Thereafter, he spent most of his time in the ubiquitous taverns, talking with the "proletariat," gathering material for his writing. He habitually came home drunk to fall senselessly into bed, sometimes urinating in his sleep (leaving me to the brutal clean-up, like a caregiver). He alternated between weeks in this mode and periods of complete sobriety, writing vehemently in his office, living on coffee, demanding no interruption.

Some young Quebecoise publishers were excited by his work, so he now had a book deadline. It was to be a collection of his impressions from his "social animation" research in California, a collage of stories, poems, word-play, photos — "revolutionary" even in format. The front cover was an enlarged photo I had taken of Patrick standing in front of native rock cliff paintings in the Arizona Painted Desert, with simply his name at the top. The back cover was another large photo, posed in Berkeley with his typical accoutrements — copies of film periodicals and revolution-ary tracts, his omnipresent cigar, jewelry and half-full gallon of red wine. Only here did we see the printed title in all lower case "Irish coffees au no name bar & vin rouge valley of the moon." For good measure the table of contents was found at the back of the book, and an afterword listed the dates of our arrival in Montreal, our arrests, and our mar-riage on April 22, 1971.

During that year before the book was published, we attended every opening of every art event, film debut, con-cert, poetry reading, etc. I was doing macrame (necklaces, lampshades, plant hangers, curtains) as my own artistic outlet and within Patrick's circle found patrons. We were frequent guests at the home of the beautiful and vivacious singer Pauline Julien, who was especially fond of three-and-a-half-year-old Serena. My impish daughter was both gregarious and articulate and often stole the show at these long gourmet luncheons. I was quite proud of her, as I was still a little shy and reticent in the company of these French-Canadian luminaries.

Pauline employed me to collaborate with her designer, Francois Barbeau, to fabricate some very fine details for her upcoming concert wardrobe. The custom belt and button coverings required many spools of silk thread and took me into the realm of lace-making. This same designer also hired me to create a bed canopy of white clothesline cord for his theater set for *Our Lady of the Camellias*. The entire play centered around this stunning bed.

New Mom 1967. Dhyanis, Serena

Serena's First Birthday 1968

Single Mom 1969

Golden Gate Park, San Francisco, 1970

Patrick Straram, writer, film critic, radio personality, 1970

Women's Lib

"The only way for a woman, as for a man, to find herself, to know herself as a person, is by creative work of her own. There is no other way." Betty Friedan

I had attended a French-Canadian Women's Lib group but found the sophisticated level of French beyond my scope and switched over to an English-speaking group. We discussed Doris Lessing's somewhat autobiographical novel *The Golden Notebook*, which daringly explored the inner lives of women who eschewed marriage in favor of pursuing their own intellectual interests. We were indignant to learn that one of our member's mother had been labeled a "narcissistic manipulator" for trying to get her needs met in trying to establish an identity outside her familial role.

We studied Simone de Beauvoir's *The Second Sex*, written in 1949 as a handbook of feminist theory. And we read the story of F. Scott Fitzgerald's wife, *Zelda: A Biography*, by Nancy Milford. We could relate to this vital, talented woman who was told not to write (compete) by her famous husband, and who was eventually driven to emotional disintegration.

At these meetings I met the lovely woman who had inspired Leonard Cohen's evocative ballad "Suzanne." She told us that he had urged her to learn the ways of the Geisha he had met in Japan, for example, always sliding his cup of tea silently from the left side. We considered this to be excessively subjugating behavior, though we admired her natural grace.

Leonard Cohen was the top poet-singer-songwriter of Canada, older and sexily marked by experience (like Patrick). It was an eye-opener to hear something about his personal life. His stanzas from that iconic song were embedded as part of our generation's folk-rock soundtrack, since first sung by Judy Collins in 1966; every self-respecting Joan Baez/Judy Collins wannabe had this in her guitar repertoire (I was one of these).

> Suzanne takes you down to her place near the river
> You can hear the boats go by
> You can spend the night beside her
> And you know that she's half-crazy
> But that's why you want to be there
> And she feeds you tea and oranges
> That come all the way from China
> And just when you mean to tell her
> That you have no love to give her
> Then she gets you on her wavelength
> And she lets the river answer
> That you've always been her lover
>
> And you want to travel with her
> And you want to travel blind
> And you know that she will trust you
> For you've touched her perfect body with your mind.

All of this Women's Liberation "consciousness raising" influence helped me realize I did not enjoy *la vie quotidienne*, daily life, with Patrick. I could sympathize with his causes and admire him as a prominent activist and literary figure, but domesticity was not his thing. Also, the prestige of being "Patrick's Woman" had worn thin and I was not so happy always appearing at events in his shadow. In spite of pleas from his friends to stay, I knew it was not working for me or for my daughter, who mostly ignored Patrick. Thus the last line of his book, the debut of which I *did* attend, reads "Unable to support life with me, she moved out on May 1st, 1972." Living apart, we remained quite friendly, and in a letter written five years later he expressed our mutual importance to each other:

"I'm convinced our meeting was great and useful. I gained a lot being with you — I believe you gained some being with me...I would enjoy talking and talking a few days and nights with you — you?"

Barbara

*"We are most nearly ourselves when we achieve the serious-
ness of a child at play." Heraclitus (535 - 474 BC)*

When I did leave, it was to move a mere few blocks away on
the same street in this adopted bilingual city of Montreal. I
got a job through Patrick's ex-girlfriend (who had left him
in California). Miliscka had taken me under her wing and
become a good friend. I worked at a government-funded
day program teaching art, including macrame and fabric
collage, to the unemployed and elderly clients, basically
the unemployed teaching the unemployed! There was free
daycare at the center where Serena made friends, and the
workshop was always full of interesting people.

Enter Barbara, an artist from England with twinkly blue
eyes and a softly rounded, curvy body. She was in Canada
to visit her brother who worked at McGill University as a
professor of entomology, or the art of organic farming using
nature's beneficial insects to control the detrimental ones in
lieu of poisonous pesticides. She stayed with his family and
also found work at this same program. Her dry Brit humor,
creativity, and overflowing compassion for everyone, especially Serena, hooked me in. We got along so well I invited
her to live with us.

The apartment instantly became a beehive of art projects. Barbara made some of her own dyes from boiled vegetables (onion skin, beetroot, etc.) and there were pots of dyes and wax for batik all over the kitchen. In the "living room," I had loops of jute or colored twine suspended to knot into lamp shades or wall hangings. We both embroidered scenes on garments and bags for our friends, sometimes on the cuffs of jeans or the entire back of a denim jacket. Serena joined in the artistic fun — I took a photo of her getting ready to dip into the bathtub, her little body completely covered in fanciful colored flow pen drawings. I sent home to my parents a painting of her kneeling on a chair, engrossed in a painting of her own.

We enjoyed Barbara's expressions; whenever something was potentially frustrating, she would liltingly say, "Don't get your knickers in a knot dahlin." We enjoyed the luxury of exploring Montreal and its rich multi-cultural layers. We made friends with the old Jewish fabric sellers in their jumbled shops along Boulevard Saint Laurent. I took French classes, attended dance workshops and literally danced my way along neighborhood sidewalks, feeling happy and free.

It was then that I met Eric, an intriguing Panamanian who had left a numbing job driving New York subway trains to study art at McGill University. I admired his sensually abstract renderings of the human form and we became "a thing." Barbara also had a steady beau and since the only doors in our apartment were cloth curtains, we were privy to the sounds of each other's nocturnal escapades. She said to me once, "You seem to have that part of life sorted out."

She did not count me among the typical Americans she had met, so often absorbed with their own psychological dramas and emotional hang-ups. I introduced her to Patrick, with whom she enjoyed a little "dilly dally." When her six-month visitor visa expired, she returned to England and we carried on an enthusiastic journal-like correspondence.

More often now Serena and I spent time with friends at Eric's more spacious flat, concocting communal rice curries, playing chess, and dancing. He told stories of travel around Europe and to India and Nepal. Winter in Quebec confined everyone to indoor activities. One friend taught me how to read Tarot cards. There were several conscientious objectors, more commonly known as draft dodgers, from America in the group with whom we exchanged guitar riffs.

Eric occasionally took Serena ice skating, and with another single mom who lived in my apartment block, we took the kids tobogganing on the hill at Parc Mont Royal. With the two young girls lined up in front, my friend lost control and the toboggan slammed into the chain link fence at the bottom of the hill. A raw edge of the strong metal slashed Serena's forehead. I had been taking photos and ran to the girls, horrified to watch Serena's wound stretch open and blood pour down her face. I used my neck scarf to pinch it together while my friend hailed a taxi. My parents had recently been to visit us, and on the way to the hospital Serena said melodramatically, "If I die, tell Grandma I love her." This panicked me even more, and I wondered how she could know something like that? However, the doctor on duty stitched her up so expertly there was no noticeable scar. This was our first test of the Canadian Healthcare System which was both free and highly effective.

Montreal also boasts a comprehensive public transportation network, with its clean underground Metro and frequent bus service. One night that spring my neighbor (the gracious afro American, Carolyn from Detroit) watched our kids while I took the bus to meet some dance enthusiast friends at The Black Cat nightclub. There the DJ played all our favorites from George Benson, Barry White, Marvin Gaye, etc.

At the end of the night everyone dispersed, leaving me to wait at the bus stop a few blocks away. A red car circled around a few times and I ignored the come-on from the young Quebecois man driving. He parked in a deserted lot, got out and grabbed me from behind, twisting my arm and squeezing my neck, forcing me into his car. He gave the impression of being well-muscled and powerfully strong, so I decided to stop struggling and speak soothingly (in French) to calm him down. Remembering how I survived some violent scenes with my first husband, I opted for "playing possum" and went limp. The only goal of the moment was not to be killed, but as he "did his thing," he started choking me to get more of a reaction, leaving purple bruises on my neck. All I could think of was getting back to Serena. Afterward he asked where he could drive me. I directed him to my general neighborhood, waited for him to disappear, then ran to my neighbor's to collapse into convulsing sobs.

For some weeks I could not sleep, lying awake shivering with fear and anger at being violated, as the shock wore off. I did not feel safe walking, fearful that the red car would turn up again. I decided to take action and make a report to the police, and they were salacious at the interview, practically drooling at every detail. This only intensified my angst! They called me in to select from a line-up, saying they had caught the same fellow raping other girls. I honestly could not recognize the perpetrator, which now made the police angry. Apparently the line-up consisted of the culprit and a host of plain clothes police, and the one I pointed out was on the force. They accused me of being deliberately uncooperative because, they said, my husband was a revolutionary.

In fact, when I spoke about this incident to Patrick, he chided me for doing the bourgeois thing by going to the "male-chauvinist fascist pigs," adding he did not appreciate them knocking at his door during their investigation. They certainly did not make me feel any better, with their attitude of "you asked for it."

One of Patrick's friends owned a multi-story pub-restaurant with gallery space for artists. I was busy preparing many large pieces to display there, including a fully hand-knotted dress of various purple yarns, very "danceable," for myself to wear at the opening reception. My "boyfriend" Eric announced out of the blue that he was leaving for Panama to see his ill father before he died. I had hoped he would stay for my opening, but he took off the week before.

Although my ex, Patrick (who now had a new paramour), and other friends were there at the reception, I felt a bit abandoned and alone. Sales went well — the owner's wife bought the largest hanging. Among the guests I met a fellow who planned to live on a communal farm in the Laurentian Mountains. He was a single dad with a young son and said there were other children there as well, ideal for Serena and me for the summer. Barbara's former "main squeeze" was happy to take over the Esplanade apartment and off we went.

The reality was far from ideal. One hippie guy laid around all day in the darkened living room saying that his job was "to think." The wife of the legitimate tenant of the farm-house had split for Florida leaving her husband and two children to fend for themselves, so it was his idea to open the place up as a commune. I became the chief cook, maid, and child-care provider for the rather slovenly lot. I felt like Wendy with the Lost Boys in *Peter Pan*. A couple of months later the wife returned with two more guys tagging after her (who moved into the chicken shed and slashed away at an electric guitar all day). When the landowners discovered that one of the bunch had cut down trees to build himself a traditional teepee, he was irate and we were disbanded. Serena and I were taken in by a French-Canadian girlfriend, another single mom, living in a nearby village.

All the while, Barbara and I had been corresponding, both unhappy with our current circumstances. We conspired to change everything; she returned to Canada and we embarked on our "journey of 10,000 miles."

Sewing a Puppet with Serena 1970

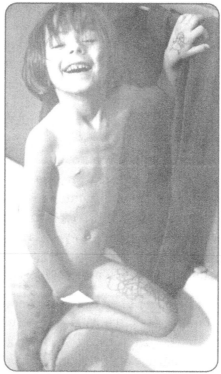

Serena's Body Art, Montreal 1972

Serena on Montreal ice 1972

Eric of Panama in Montreal 1972

Barbara of England with Serena 1973

Purple Yarn Macrame Dress 1973

Macrame Suspended Bed, Montreal Theater 1972

10,000-Mile Journey

"As I unclutter my life, I free myself to answer the callings of my soul." Wayne Dyer

Seeking a change from the predictable challenges of struggling artists in Western Civilization (her England, my North America, our Canada), we left Montreal for the open road. In the autumn of 1973 British artist and dear friend Barbara, myself, and five-year-old daughter Serena — "The Witches Three" set off hitchhiking to Mexico. We hoped for both warmer temperatures and a more favorable economic climate for survival by art. Both Barbara and I dreamed of becoming self-sustaining artists in a place where the cost of materials did not surpass the market price of the final product. But this quest was a bit like The Fool card in the Tarot deck — jumping off a cliff into space with nothing but faith that the universe would provide a safety net!

I bestowed my "valuables" to a few friends; the indispensable second-hand fur coat that had protected me through three long Quebec winters and the contents of my shabby-chic apartment were no longer needed. I stitched together a Navy-style canvas duffel bag for our few essentials, a mini backpack for Serena, and slung my guitar over one shoulder. The loose plan was to visit an art school friend of Barb's in Toronto, then look up a couple I knew from San Francisco now relocated in Victoria, B.C., and from there hitch down the West Coast to stop at my family's home before embarking for our ultimate destination, south of the border.

We spent that first night on the floor of Barb's hospitable chum's flat, then set out the following morning with that elated feeling of infinite possibility. Barbara liked to say, as we waited beside the road watching cars speed past, "Our next ride is just having their breakfast." And, magically, our very next ride was headed all the way to Vancouver! The two fellows were delivering this car cross country. One drove while the other slept in the passenger seat, taking shifts, pausing only for meals at truck stops. They called themselves "Happy" and "Lucky," which corresponded with our mood. We passed our snacks, offered neck massages from the back seat, slept some and kept up a cheerful banter as the miles whizzed by with these very kind gentlemen.

We found the bucolic Vancouver Island property of my friends, "Silk" and "Duv," whom I had met while working at the ad agency in San Francisco during my first years as a single mother (1968-69). They had dubbed me "Lady Madonna," after the Beatles' song and taken me on many weekend excursions into the country with Serena. They had introduced me to the gentle psychedelic drug mescaline, derived from psychoactive cactus. The recreational drug culture had been burgeoning while I was sequestered away dealing with the domestic problems of young marriage and a newborn, and Silk helped me to catch up and join in.

Back then we had camped together in the Valley of the Moon (Sonoma) on their friend's land near a picturesque pond. While floating on my back under the influence of mescaline and gazing at the sky, the soft clouds above formed themselves into kaleidoscopic pastel paisley patterns. During a subsequent "trip" we took in the Sierras, walking through the woods, I felt "inhabited" by a Native American. The altered state allowed me to walk soundlessly without the crackling of a single leaf or twig. I thought I could see the plant "devas" and commune with the sweet spirits of each insect, bird, and reptile. I had not felt frightened or out of control, only a heightened awareness and surrender to this expanded consciousness. While these impressions are difficult to articulate, they remain forever ingrained as small windows into the vast unseen. Everything is perceived as vibrating interconnected energy, and there is a temporary release from the illusion of separation.

Although I never bought a single drug, they were ubiquitous in this time of "sex, drugs, rock n' roll," so I sampled many. Free concerts in Haight-Ashbury and Golden Gate Park were walking distance from my San Francisco apartment. Everyone brought their kids and Serena rode on my shoulders to these Love-ins, where everyone got along, whether high or not.

I saw others become addicted to various substances — it was impossible not to inhale marijuana particulates everywhere — but I felt like having the responsibility of motherhood kept me grounded and not at all tempted to float away into drug-induced oblivion. Not so for everyone — I had one roommate with a small son whom I thought would be the perfect live-in babysitter. Several times I came home to find her in a semi-conscious state in her bed with the kids unattended. I discovered her boyfriend was bringing her heroine and sorrowfully, had to ask her to leave.

The apartment was in the center of a poor ghetto-type neighborhood and I said cheerful hellos to anyone who passed as we occasionally sat on the front stoop. One night one of these casual acquaintances climbed the fire escape up to my third-story bedroom window and blithely appeared, asking me to tie off his arm so he could shoot up. This dude spent the next few hours expounding on a vision — his musical group would change the world led by him, the next incarnation of Jesus Christ. My angels were on duty that night, protecting us and keeping him harmless, as I was well aware drugs could prove otherwise.

Now, after hitchhiking to Vancouver in 1973, we spent a few pleasant days catching up with the talented Silk's graphic business and hearing of their plans to build their own boat and sail off into the sunset. At this time President Richard Nixon was involved with the Watergate scandal, and many of us were disgusted with the corruption in American politics.

We, the three witches, followed the coastal highway south through Washington and Oregon to California, enjoying the exhilarating scenery. We had been dropped off in Coos Bay, Oregon, with its wild cliffs and rocky little islands rising up out of the sea, forming breathtaking skyscapes. The locals in each area who picked us up were friendly and interested in our free-flowing travels. Barbara proudly proclaimed that she was descended from the Lancashire Witches and retained great powers of manifestation. It seemed we were all three tuned in to the universal law that "intention summons circumstance" and felt safe and guided in our progress along the road.

Witches heed the childlike right brain, ever open to ordinary magic and enchantment. This included Serena with her focused "fresh eyes," who seemed a powerful little accomplice. We never lacked for the next ride, or meal, or moment of synchronous wonder as we headed towards our next stop on the way to the Mexican border — a visit to my family and the San Francisco Bay Area where I had been born and raised.

Flashback City

"True forgiveness is when you can say 'Thank you for that experience'." Oprah Winfrey

Barbara and I, with Serena, had arranged to stay in a shared house in Oakland, city of my birth through high school graduation. My former Panamanian boyfriend Eric (who had been studying art in Montreal) coincidentally now lived there with several roommates. One of these was a well-known experimental choreographer whose show we witnessed. It was actually not choreographed at all but a psychological angst-ridden in-the-moment movement improvisation, prompted by shouted word triggers. It was supposed to be avant-garde, but I found it too heady for my more sensual dance aesthetic.

The last time I had seen Eric was when he had left Montreal to visit his ill father in Panama but perhaps also to escape our taken-for-granted relationship. I had been about to open an exhibit of my large macrame installations, but he had not stayed for the occasion and simply exited my life in the most amicable way. Although I had felt abandoned and alone at the show reception, I always thought of our relationship with nostalgia. Now it was clear our attraction was downgraded to just friends. I cheerfully gave him my guitar, having found it too cumbersome for our mode of travel.

In Oakland while out for lunch with Barbara and Serena, I was surprised to recognize an important figure from my past — my very first lover, Jack. Years ago he had been living in Berkeley but followed me to hang out in Santa Barbara where I was attending my second year at UCSB. I was living in a dorm and used to cycle off campus to bring him food in my pocket from the dorm cafeteria. He was not working but spent the days playing guitar while he crashed at a friend's apartment. He embodied the cynical lyrics of Bob Dylan, whom my father had rightly dubbed subversive, living the life of the glorified "rolling stone." He was funny and taught me about music and was content to hang out and carry on our chaste love affair. That is, until I chose between the Catholic doctrine and sex, nearly insisting we go all the way. Directly after that one time, which did not seem like anything special to me, he inexplicably disappeared — without a word.

This was a shock since I had in my mind we would marry. When I mentioned this to a male friend in drawing class, he asked, "Why would you want to do that?" Though in 1965 the rigid (and to our generation hypocritical) mores were loosening and divorce was on the rise, I was still tied to societal expectations. Unmarried people did not yet live together without scandal. Also I think I saw marriage as synonymous with adulthood and freedom from parental authority. After he left I was absorbed more and more by the bohemian element on campus, joining candlelight vigils on the library steps to protest the Vietnam War and identifying with the folksingers at the student union.

At summer break back with my parents in Oakland, I had borrowed the family car to look for a job. But first since I hadn't yet given up on Jack, I tracked him down in Berkeley. He acted withdrawn and depressed (perhaps on drugs, of which I was ignorant). He claimed I even kissed differently. He took me to my first psychedelic concert at the Avalon Ballroom in San Francisco with a light show — Big Brother and the Holding Company and Jefferson Airplane — and to a Berkeley cafe to hear Country Joe and The Fish sing their ironic anti-war songs. But when we met one morning for coffee while I scanned the want-ads for a suitable job, he suggested we cross Telegraph Avenue to the supermarket for cigarettes. He hastily stuffed a carton under my poncho before we nonchalantly paid for a thirty-nine-cent package of sweet rolls. Exiting the store I heard, "Young lady, didn't you forget something?" and I was hauled off to the city jail. Jack went to borrow $50 for bail and I was put in a room equipped with a typewriter, where I reeled off an angry piece of "Beat" poetry, understanding that our relationship had reached a dead end.

Now at our chance encounter years later, I asked Jack what was up with all that. He explained that at our one-time union he had discovered that I was not a virgin and that I had lied to him. He *still* refused to believe that he was in fact my first. I cannot explain why he concluded that, but I mumbled something about falling off a horse. Although I had nothing to compare him to at the time, he was a fairly small man...!?

I invited Barbara and my good friend Panamanian Eric to our family's Thanksgiving dinner. I considered him a well-traveled, cultured artist. My mother, however, was so put off by him she called him "the devil." I did not understand that extreme reaction and chalked it up to knee-jerk racism as this was the first black person I was aware of ever to sit at her table. Of course I could not blame her for being wary of anyone I brought around or for being displeased about my seemingly unfocused, nomadic lifestyle. Probably for Serena's sake my parents mostly refrained from criticism, though I'm sure their tongues often "suffered teeth marks." The one time they had visited us in Montreal, they left me with "You are doing a good job raising your daughter." Certainly my hippie style of parenthood was deliberately the opposite of theirs, stressing freedom over restriction. Serena was articulate and well-adjusted even at age 4, probably by nature and not so much thanks to me, although I did my best to show her love, provide a sense of security, and instill good manners.

I paid a visit to Jim's mother as a courtesy for her to see her grandchild. She was cold to me, believing Jim's explanation that I had left him back in 1968 for a new boyfriend. We arranged to have Jim also see Serena. He was restored to his former happy-go-lucky-guy demeanor, telling me he had no idea what had gotten into him during our marriage. Barbara even "had a diddle" with him, finding him amusing and pleasant. I would never trust him again but had long since forgiven him and let the past go.

I began to think that my karma in this life is one of *completion*, perhaps of past life relationships. It appeared that at this moment I had fully completed my relationships with Jack, Jim, Patrick, and Eric, each of which had felt so compelling and inevitable in their own time, as if we had unfinished business to settle.

On the Road Again

"...Follow your heart even when it leads you off the well-worn path, and that will make all the difference."
Steve Jobs

Wrapping up our Bay Area visit, in preparation for our intended journey, we three witches all had our high-maintenance long hair chopped off at a men's barber shop and set off south again around Christmas. One objective we had along the way was to see the Watts Towers of Simon Rodia in the low-income L.A. neighborhood of Watts.

This is a cluster of tall sculptural structures enclosed in a small triangle of land. The sign there says they were "painstakingly constructed from society's leftovers," and they are all embedded with gorgeous mosaics of broken bits of tile, ceramics, and bottle glass. They took 30 years to build by this one man as a labor of love and have been preserved as an inspiring local landmark.

We also stopped at the La Brea Tar Pits for a picnic on the grounds where natural asphalt seeped up and preserved the bones of Ice Age animals like a saber-tooth tiger and a giant behemoth.

Barbara thought to call the local Quakers, whom she had heard always take in traveling strangers, no questions asked.

This proved true; we were put up for the night in a nice suburban home on the outskirts of the L.A. jungle. From there we hitched to the home of more of my relatives, an aunt and uncle in Chula Vista, close to the Mexican border. We were treated to plentiful leftovers from their Christmas turkey dinner, along with some uncomfortable conversation regarding our "plans." It was to be our last night in proper beds for many moons to come!

Baja

"It may be that when we no longer know which way to go,
we have come to our real journey." Wendell Berry

As it happened, we were on foot, crossing from the U.S. to
Mexico via a pedestrian passage without any customs kiosks
or immigration officials to stamp our passports. We must
have been considered day visitors. Such relaxed border
crossings could never happen today, but we gave it not one
thought as we blithely headed into Baja.

Along the road was a palm-thatch covered area where
women were patting out tortillas. They let us try, laughing
heartily until we caught the rhythm of working the ball of
masa with our palms into a flat disc ready for toasting on
the smoky fire-fueled griddles. That culinary lesson was to
serve us well. We were encouraged by our instant connection with these happy, friendly, open people and felt giddy
with the newness and adventure.

We hitched a ride out of Tijuana to Rosarito where we set
up our first camp on a wide beach, pitching our little orange
nylon tent nestled in the lee of the cliffs. We ate a dinner
of sliced *jicama*, a new vegetable for us, talked to some
Mexicans who gave us permission to stay there, and settled
into the tent shortly after sunset. Then began a torrential
rain and we found ourselves in the path of a flash flood. We
were in an *arroyo*, or stream bed that collected rain from

the cliffs above, forming a river to the beach and practically floating us away.

Atop those cliffs there was a trailer park where our bedraggled trio knocked on the door of the only unit with lights still on. An American woman sheltered us for the rest of the night, and we added the word *arroyo* to our Mexican vocabulary! When we reached Ensenada, we were more careful picking our beach campsite. There we had the obligatory drink at the legendary Hussong's Cafe. We sampled the delicious classic Mexican hot chocolate laced with cinnamon, but the place was filled with expats who mostly ignored us and we moved on.

We had only the vaguest notion of the topography or mileage between towns, or how far to the tip of the peninsula. We measured our progress only by direct experience of each small outpost, the landscapes, and the people who offered us rides, often in the back of ramshackle pickup trucks. We delighted in our fledgling attempts to communicate in Spanish. One family let us off at dusk in the desert where the highway crosses the land from the Pacific Ocean to the eastern gulf shore. We gathered dry skeletons of saguaro cactus for a campfire. As the flames caught, we were surprised to see several scorpions fleeing out of the basketweave holes in the hollow "logs." We began to respect the intense life of the desert.

Soon we came upon the white sand oasis of Mulege (pronounced *Mu*-la-hay) for a cleansing swim in the blue water of the Gulf of California. A few hippie campers imparted their knowledge of a friendly beach farther south near the town of La Paz. We pressed on, sometimes walking and singing or catching a ride for a few miles — the three witches, our novel robust group of two young women and a cheerful five-year-old. We reached Pichilingi Beach, which became our base camp for a few weeks. Clams were prolific, there for the easy digging along the shallow shore, and we kept a large pot of chowder going over our campfire. The local shrimp boat fishermen sometimes came ashore and contributed random fish caught in their nets. It must be said that cooking was one of Barbara's high arts and she could make gourmet meals from the humblest ingredients; for example, a luxurious bisque from discarded shrimp heads.

Occasionally we made the hike into town for vegetables, tins of evaporated milk, corn *masa* for tortillas and other supplies. There we met the captains and crews of sailboats moored in the La Paz harbor. One was the pirate-looking, black-hulled "Sylvia" onto which we were welcomed aboard by the swashbuckling Captain Ted. We talked and swigged *Rompope*, a creamy yellow eggnog-like rum concoction, discussing politics and his outlaw lifestyle into the night. I was infatuated with him, but he was only interested in women who could help crew his next voyage. I wrote an angst-ridden poem to him and told him sentimentally to look me up if he ever sailed into San Francisco Bay.

On the beach we had become the unofficial hostesses, welcoming new campers who arrived via the nearby ferry. We always offered a cup of hearty chowder, sharing our evening campfire with music, camaraderie, and the omnipresent *mezcal*. This strong clear alcohol is distilled from Agave, or *Maguey*, cactus and is like the moonshine version of tequila — with a higher alcohol content to pack a real punch! One day a group of yuppies from Marin County, where my family now lived on the San Rafael Canal, visited our camp. They were fascinated by us and invited us to spend a night at their rented villa. We were happy to use the impressive open tile shower, enjoy a sumptuous barbeque, and bond with these lovely people. Upon my return to Marin more than a year later, I looked them up and we became good friends.

One day I ventured into town with Serena, leaving Barbara at the beach. An immigration officer asked to see my passport, which he sternly pointed out had no entry stamp. I did not involve Barbara, but we two were ordered back to the Tijuana border to obtain the stamps. I hitchhiked with Serena back to my aunt and uncle in Chula Vista to borrow $100 cash, which I promised to repay later. Serena and I retraced the road to La Paz where Barbara had struck up a romance with one of the shrimp fishermen. His boat was due to head home across the gulf to Guaymas on the mainland of Mexico.

She decided to accompany him, while I arranged a ride with another of the sailboat crews, this one from Canada, who were also ready to sail, but to Matzatlan south of Guaymas where Barb and I planned to meet up. The lovely boat was called "Turquoise" and the flirtatious divorcee captain was happy to have a galley cook and bunkmate.

Sexual freedom was the norm, as common as a handshake, and no one was hung up about it; it was one thing about Women's Liberation that men appreciated! I had long since adopted this attitude and found ways to "love the one you're with" (popular lyric from Stephen Stills' 1970 song by that title). This was quite a big change from the "happily ever after with one person" Disney fairy tale instilled in my generation from the early fifties.

Beneath all the cavalier sexual encounters I experienced, there still lurked an undercurrent of hope for Prince Charming to appear, to love for all time — someone who could truly understand and appreciate my qualities and want to protect and keep me "happily ever after." But this secret desire was considered bourgeois, not really acknowledged, and deeply buried in favor of the "bon vivant" lifestyle. And there was strong peer pressure to NOT appear uptight.

Thus, this captain and I laughed and cavorted like happy puppies on the short voyage. Though I had been indifferent to my family's sailing mania, I had to admit those three days crossing the gulf were a glorious sailing experience. The weather was fine and when I cooked the fresh *bonito* (diminutive tuna) caught by the crew, it was beyond delectable. Dolphins frolicked alongside us in the foamy wake by day and in green sparkling phosphorescence by night. I traveled with an omnipresent stash of art supplies, so I created string and glass bead macrame décor for the light sconces below deck as part of my passage. Someone came up with the name Handmades Underway for my marine macrame line.

I made diary entries, wrote a couple of poems, and started reading The First Circle by Aleksandr Solzhenitsyn. I was preoccupied by his struggle against dogmatism and his defense of allowing thoughts to develop naturally: "Books and other people's opinions are shears which sever the life of a thought. One must first come upon the thought oneself; later on one can verify it in a book." Of course this was further corroboration of the experimental life I was choosing over finishing my abandoned university degree!

New Visas

"If we recognize that change and uncertainty are basic principles, we can greet the future and the transformation we are undergoing with the understanding that we do not know enough to be pessimistic." Hazel Henderson

From the Mazatlan dock I found a cheap youth hostel in town, not knowing how or when we would meet up with Barbara who was coming by land from Guaymas. Serena and I walked up the hill to the top of the high cliffs to watch the famous daredevil Mexican youths swan dive through the air to the ocean pool so far below. *Muy Peligroso!* Even more amazing than this performance, as we turned down the hill, we came face to face with our "mate" Barbara! Reunited, we seamlessly continued the trek south. Between rides were stretches of walking in the heat of the day. Sometimes we picked tamarinds from overhanging trees, sucking the tart fruit for refreshment and hoping we would not be considered thieves.

The Canadians planned to dock at Puerto Vallarta for an upcoming fiesta and invited us should we happen to arrive there in time. We stopped just north of P.V. at a less populated fishing community known as La Penita. A dirt track cut through a thin forest, past a few basic cement block houses, and led to the beach. One of the houses was an unfinished and uninhabited shell with a roof and along the walls two cement platforms we used as beds. We camped and explored the immediate area to find no other tourists, but one trail led to a small bakery that turned out delicious fragrant flour rolls and pan dulce, slightly sweetened puffy round treats.

The baker's son, Javier, a tall, lithe, handsome Mestizo (mixed blood - Indio and Spanish) with smooth cafe-au-lait skin attached himself to our party, declaring, "You girls need a guide." Since my new passport stamp was good for only one month which dwindled day by day and Barbara still had a blank book, we had decided to traverse the length of Mexico and cross over the southern border into Guatemala. Javier told us we could obtain a coveted six-month visa upon returning to Mexico from the south. Finding a charming indigenous guide for this journey seemed like more of the good fortune we always optimistically expected as the three witches, so we accepted his offer. Javier spoke fluent English and was generous both with translation and teaching us the language. He had "style," and I dubbed him (still carrying Patrick's influence) *Aguila de la Montana*, or Eagle of the Mountain.

He moved in with us and I found he was a notably good lover. He fit that rare combination of a body and rhythms perfectly matched to mine. Barbara made sketches of us intertwined and decades later sent me a watercolor from that batch of drawings. This all evolved over a few weeks while Javier pre-pared his family for his imminent departure from his role at the bakery. And before we embarked, Javier murmured to me that I "could teach him a lot about love." That might be a good indication of how slick our new friend was. I have probably never heard a better line — in any language — well, it got me! We were both Aquarians, though he was a couple of years younger than my "older woman" age of just-turned-26.

During that time the witches three made one sojourn into the larger town. What I recall most vividly from the views of

Puerto Vallarta in 1974 were everywhere the bright splashes of purple and red bougainvillea clinging to whitewashed walls crowding up the hillsides overlooking the pristine bay.

I also met up with the Canadians at the harbor, pre-partying on the boat with bottles of tequila. Embarrassingly, I must have passed out in a bunk and awoke later to find everyone gone — and that I had completely missed the fiesta. When I returned to La Penita the next day, Barbara told me she and Javier had "had a diddle." Though sharing partners was not unusual, still, I felt a jealous pang. To assuage those old feelings of insecurity, I asked Javier how he had felt about it. He said, "The contact was good." I knew by now how nurturing were Barbara's full-breasted hugs. She was a wonderful second mother to Serena, who also loved her cuddles. But as far as I knew, she and Javier never "diddled" again and I let go of my involuntary possessive reaction.

We set out again southward all together and when he could, Javier offered his skills to help out a local fisherman or baker. In exchange the family took us girls into their small home to eat and sleep while he worked through the night producing the next day's freshly baked goods. We thought, "What a gem!". We stopped briefly in the wildly colorful market town of Guadalajara and actually stayed in a modest hotel so we could shower and explore the *zocalo*, or main square, and its vendors. We savored the local *tacos de cabeza*, or slow-roasted beef head tacos. Oh, and the heavenly *flan*! The next day we got a ride in a meat truck on its way to Mexico City and that night we slept in an empty meat trailer, pungent with the raw smell of blood.

Along the coast of Oaxaca, we camped at Puerto Angel beach and Javier was extremely friendly with other foreign adventurers. At the border town of Tehuantepec, in the southernmost state of Chiapas, we bunked in at a *pension* before crossing into Guatemala on a crowded, rickety bus. I recall a harrowing ride through a mountainous dense jungle rain. At one point the bus stopped where a landslide had, minutes before, blocked the road. We all trudged over the mud to board another bus on the other side. It was cold and damp, and the people were bundled in knit caps and bright sweaters, inhabiting small houses that resembled stone igloos with smoke streaming from holes in the roofs. We were anxious to return to Mexico with our fresh six-month visas and wherever fate would take us.

Oaxaca

"Loss is the uninvited door that extends us an unexpected invitation to unimaginable possibilities."
Craig D. Lounsbrough

We had no clue that Javier might have an ulterior motive for accompanying us south. He knew we were on a shoestring budget when we arrived in Oaxaca City. We went straight to Rosalia's Health Food Store and Cafe, which catered to hippie travelers and expats. Javier appealed to this bold, bigger-than-life woman for a place to stay. Probably the presence of Serena softened her heart, and she offered us an empty cement block structure on land she owned at the eastern outskirts of town near El Tule.

This was planted with various fruit tree seedlings that needed watering, so we were allowed to use the dwelling in exchange for the daily labor of filling buckets with water from the one spigot and carrying it to each young sapling. We swept out the debris and made ourselves comfortable in the primitive two-room house happily tending the trees. Down the road we visited a landmark tree, a Montezuma Cypress with the stoutest trunk in the world. The El Tule tree is over 1,400 years old with a girth of 137 feet.

Meanwhile, Javier would disappear for a few days apparently engaged in his own enterprise, of which we knew nothing. Suddenly, he reappeared saying we were asked to leave. It seemed that Rosalia had caught wind that Javier was involved in buying and selling marijuana (illegal at that time) and wanted us gone. He took us on a bus, crowded with chicken coups and black curly-haired pigs, over the mountain range and back to the coast and friends of his who lived in a humble hut in a very small village. This was most likely Javier's drug connection; the couple seemed highly sophisticated for this subsistence farmer environment, but marijuana was likely the most profitable crop and they were the distribution conduit. Honestly, the three witches remained innocent of whatever deals were going on, but we loved the place, La Barra de Colotepec.

As I was still making small macrame jewelry items to sell, Javier took a few to the tourist beach seven kilometers down the road at Puerto Escondido. He said he would tell the hippies the bracelets and necklaces were made by the native *Cacahuate Indios* (translation "Peanut Indians"). He returned with welcome food supplies from the market there. Immediately afterwards I could not find in my duffel bag the expensive Nikon camera my father had loaned me for the trip. I was starting to suspect Javier of all around deceit. Strong marijuana joints were passed, and another young American woman who hung out with us commented to Barbara that I appeared frightened. I felt quite duped when I realized that Javier had stolen and sold the camera, and though I did not think of myself as generally "frightened," in fact did become withdrawn in the company of these people.

Before Javier left us there, we met Juan, a young man who was caretaker of an empty house on a hill across the river (the village straddled both sides of the Colotepec River). He said we would be welcome to stay there as the absentee owner, Miguel-Angel, worked in Acapulco and visited rarely. Juan escorted us, walking across the shallow river, through a mangrove forest, and up a root-laced foot trail to the promontory overlooking the delta where the river met the sea.

The house was built of sturdy horizontal bamboo "sticks" an inch or so apart, lashed together to stronger beams at the top to support a palm thatch roof, and had a packed earthen floor. Inside was suspended a large hammock and along one wall was a stick platform which served as a typical bed. The thatch extended outside to create a shady porch area with a traditional stove, or *comal*, consisting of a raised stone platform with a metal grill. A steep trail led down to the river where we washed everything including ourselves, our few camp dishes and clothing. This seemed quite adequate and we adapted readily, learning the customs of the village through Juan, who had become sweet on Barbara.

The House of Miguel-Angel

"I long, as does every human being, to be home wherever I find myself." Maya Angelou

Although somewhat isolated on this hill, we often trekked down through the village and the seven kilometers along the highway to Puerto Escondido (Hidden Port) to the market. We met the village women walking with their leathery bare feet, transporting tall baskets of heavy bananas balanced on their heads, laughing and gossiping (probably about us).

In town we became friendly with a Canadian restaurant owner and his flamboyant Mexican wife, Aida, who knew everyone and everyone's business. She needed a sign painted on the high wall adjoining the staircase leading up to the covered open-air restaurant-bar, El Patio. I accomplished that in two-foot-high lettering, perched on a precarious ladder on the stairs. Barbara helped in the kitchen, cooking beans and salsa and baking rolls as she had learned from Javier. I tried a short stint as a waitress there but found I could not overcome the language barrier, even with an ever-increasing village vocabulary.

A rather creepy friend of Miguel-Angel came to stay at the house. He spoke English but sat around many days chatting in crass Spanish with Juan. From him we learned the repetitive swear words *pinche chingada* and *pendejo*, which he inserted multiple times into every sentence. With us he built up the mystique around the now legendary Miguel-Angel, whom I was most anxious to meet.

The day came when he did show up and accepted our residence at his abode in friendly stride. We naturally became lovers and I learned that he had spent time at the University of Michigan, though mostly experimenting with LSD rather than taking classes. He claimed he could entertain and amaze his friends by "projecting his thoughts onto a screen" and considered himself quite special with these metaphysical powers. Now, however, his "job" in Acapulco was as liaison to these same friends, escorting drug deliveries to be smuggled in small planes into the U.S.

So, these jungle farmers did indeed grow more than their obvious crops of sesame, corn, squash and beans. Apparently there were marijuana plants hidden among the sesame by the younger generation. Miguel-Angel stayed for some weeks doing his business with them. He told me of a previous girlfriend who had arrived at the village on a horse and painted a fairytale image of their love affair, saying that she would always be his "ideal." This set me to wondering if I could ever live up to this vision of perfection — maybe if I had a horse? He then left the house to us again and went off on his motorcycle back to Acapulco.

Because of the popular El Patio sign, we were asked to do more artwork around the town. The local *dentista* had built a few ocean-view bungalows and had the idea to designate each with its own East Indian name. The Beatles had been to India, and George Harrison, along with Alan Watts, Timothy Leary and Ram Dass popularized its philosophy and vernacular, which had spread even to the young and hip in Mexico. Barbara and I bought half-pint tins of primary colored enamel paints and divided up the work. My favorite was Govinda (Sanskrit for "protector of cows" referring to Krishna's youth as a cowherd, but I just liked the sound and the way the letters flowed together).

The dentist was kind to us and also prescribed topical medicine when all three of us turned up with a crazy-making case of scabies. These are microscopic burrowing insects which cause extreme itching in patches under the skin, especially active at night. Other people consistently offered a few pesos or food to trade for our artwork.

The main place for tourists to stay in town was a small beach cabana-style motel cum trailer court, dense with palm trees and strung with hammocks. We befriended a few of the steady stream of transient *gringos*. When in town we spent time at their campsites singing and swapping stories.

Two single moms with kids of Serena's age invited us to visit them in California, which we eventually did. One was living a permanently camping lifestyle in the northern county of Trinity, and the other in a small clapboard house in Santa Cruz. The world was full of single mothers and we took our responsibility for these little people seriously, though in our non-conformist way. We were simpatico for many reasons. We were choosing to raise our fatherless children away from mainstream culture, side-stepping the hyper-commercialism of the American family model.

We were far from the influence of television and macho/ glam films of the day. Making and enjoying music was one of our favorite pastimes and we did listen to the relatable feminist lyrics of women songwriters like Carole King, Joni Mitchell and Carly Simon. One of these traveling moms-on-the-beach introduced me to the astoundingly beautiful voice of country-pop star Dolly Parton who had released her album "Just Because I'm a Woman," and I became a fan.

Hurricane

"Being temporary doesn't make something matter less, because the point isn't for how long, the point is that it happened." Robyn Schneider

The next time we heard the roar of Miguel-Angel's motorcycle cutting through the tranquil village, the rainy season had begun. The river had swollen to a dangerously raging muddy torrent, threatening to sweep away everything along its banks. After days of high winds and tropical downpour, this was officially declared a hurricane, and the roads leading into Puerto Escondido were washed out, leaving the town completely cut off.

A Naval ship was deployed to deliver sacks of grain and beans to the residents. Barbara and I had been to town and were offered a ride back to the village in a helicopter, which was parked on the deck of the ship. We said yes to everything! We had to get into a small boat and scale the formidable side of the ship on a rope ladder in order to board the helicopter and ride those seven kilometers over the coastline, back to Miguel-Angel's hillside, which had a big enough clearing for the helicopter to land.

Miguel-Angel was anxious to return to Acapulco on that same ship since the roads were impassable, and he asked me to accompany him. I left Serena in Barbara's care and joined him and a few other stranded tourists for a very rough passage up the coast. We watched the crew harpoon lovely sea turtles which they then fed to us in the form of repulsive greasy, fishy patties. I was not sure if I felt seasick from the constant tossing of the ship or the fresh memory of the gory turtle massacre.

We spent a few days in Miguel-Angel's small but clean hillside apartment, descending to the beach area when the weather cleared. My impression was of unaesthetic high-rise hotels, a cluttered and littered miles-long crescent beach, and polluted water. I could not wait to get back to "our" beloved unspoiled village. But it too was damaged and changed. Although the river had receded to its normal flow, its banks were now scattered with all manner of household goods and debris from ruined structures. The trail to Miguel-Angel's house was obliterated by upended tree roots and punctuated by bright plastic items such as buckets, bowls, *bolsas* (woven market bags) half buried in the mud. However it was not long before the village pulled together and rebuilt whatever had been ravaged, and the simple life was restored to its former pragmatic pace.

Map of Baja and Mexico 1973

Ocean View from House of Miguel-Angel,
La Barra de Colotepec 1974

Three Witches in Juan's hut, La Barra
1974. D, Serena, Barbara

Serena Art with Flowers and Angel 1974. Age 6

Colotepec

*"If you lay with a scorpion, don't be surprised if it
finally stings you."* DaShanne Stokes

During the next of Miguel-Angel's absences, another gentleman caller, Antonio Cervantes, came looking for him,
and finding us there, invited us all to show him around the
three-block long town and then showered us with luxuries.
At one of our recent tortilla-and-bean breakfasts, Barbara
had beseeched the Universe, uttering how nice it would be
to have bacon and eggs. Just one day later Antonio's gifts
included a ranch breakfast of eggs, bacon and fancy cocktails. He offered to buy us whatever we wanted, and our
modest desires included blank notebooks, an embroidered
shawl, and fabric to make new dresses from the local dry
goods kiosk. We were grateful as all of this was beyond our
frugal means. We later learned that Miguel-Angel had never
heard his name, but to us he remained a mystery angel with
a famous Spanish author alias.

And who should reappear but our old friend Javier, possibly
stocking up on contraband merchandise. He observed, "You
girls have been eating too many beans. Your *culo* is getting
flabby." He invited only me into town for a healthier meal
at El Patio, which after a few shots of tequila progressed
to a whole night at the nearby inn. I'm sure everyone who

knew Miguel-Angel, including Aida, was anxious to report my loose behavior, though he and I had not agreed to any formal relationship.

When Miguel-Angel returned, he gave me a hard stare and a harder slap. Barbara had moved in with Juan, who had his own hut in his large family's compound, so I took Serena to live in another empty shack near them in the lower village. Each dwelling here had one dangling light bulb, and for plumbing a band of free-range pigs who came rushing to clean up practically before you finished your squat in the bushes. Our diets were high in corn and papaya, so even the waste made a healthy meal for those pigs.

One family operated a small tienda, consisting of a few shelves stocked with *masa*, semolina flour, soft drinks, beer, and *galletas* (animal cracker cookies) passed across the counter wrapped in newspaper by the young wife Adela. She also had the only record player, with loudspeaker, in the village and played a limited selection of popular songs. I mostly remember "*Yo Tengo Una Burra Tuerta*" (I Have a One-Eyed Female Burro) blaring through the loudspeaker at least twenty times per day. Whenever a fiesta occurred, everyone gathered there and danced to the familiar soundtrack.

From this part of the village, a well-worn trail led down to a sand and gravel beach on the riverbank. We joined the women every morning to fill our gourd water jugs. They showed us how to scrape holes in the gravel and let it seep full with naturally "filtered" water, which was surprisingly free of dysentery-causing bacteria. They used plastic scoops to fill the jug, which they then bore on their heads with impeccable posture up the trail to their respective huts. The jugs were placed on a tripod of sticks, a standard feature of every home, to be used as the daily water supply.

One morning as I entered my hut, head high, gourd pot aloft, I felt a sharp sting on one foot and saw that the culprit was a small scorpion. I had been forewarned that the remedy for a scorpion sting was a squeeze of *limon* or lime juice on the wound. It worked and as the pain subsided, for good measure I squeezed the rest of the juice onto the innocent arachnid to watch it recoil from the acid assault. Apparently it had fallen from the thatched roof above. Years later I was told by an anthropologist that the name of the village, La Barra de Colotepec, means "the barb of the scorpion" in the ancient Indian languages, including Zapoteca, and there is no translation in Spanish.

Golondrina

"Simplicity is usually the honored repository of the greatest truths. The profound and the simple are first cousins."
Norman Vincent Peale

In town I met a German tourist who had ridden a horse one hundred miles over the mountains from Oaxaca and now wanted to sell her. I returned to the village riding a skinny docile mare named *Golondrina*, or "Swallow." Having loved horses since my teen years I hold with the sentiment that "one feels a sensation of peace and quietude if one allows a horse's loving spirit to enter the human heart." This one also needed some TLC, so I kept her inside at night with us like a pet and felt more protected from the strange nocturnal sounds. I rode her up into the terraced farmlands, patches of cleared land among the dense jungle. Once she shied and refused to go further. It took a few moments for me to locate the cause of her fear, a thick dark snake dangling from a tree just ahead over the trail, and I was glad to rely on her instincts.

A family across the river requested painted designs on their rough-hewn table and benches and paid with food. They served us a *mole* so piquante I could hardly swallow, but Serena ate heartily, being more acclimated to the local fare. These folks also rented me a better adobe hut for the sum of twenty-four pesos per month — at the time about two dollars. This was where we felt most at home with a view of the river below and a little yard. Here Serena acquired a tiny white dog and a couple of chickens to tend. Golondrina now spent most of her time grazing along the river.

The local school teacher paid me a visit to ask if Serena would like to attend the little two-hut schoolhouse. This man was not indigenous but seemed to care about educating the more primitive village children. I was touched to be included and gratefully accepted. Until then Serena had no playmates during school hours; now she joined her friends in first grade and became even more proficient in Spanish. She also did lots of beautiful drawings depicting animals, people, and her favorite flowers and butterflies.

Whenever anyone caught a larger animal among the trees of the area, such as an iguana or an armadillo, it was sacrificed to a communal feast. A group of women cooked up a delicious stew which they smeared into the center of fresh sweet corn *tamales* wrapped in banana leaves and distributed to everyone, us included. We had integrated into village life and were considered less and less *extranas* (strangers), although there was still so much we did not know.

Day of the Dead

"Death reminds us that life is a temporary privilege, not an endless right." Craig D. Lounsbrough

All the villagers busily made preparations for the *Dia de los Muertos* (Day of the Dead) celebration. One hallmark food for this ritual is the special egg bread, braided into doll shapes and baked; but there was only one communal clay oven to serve the whole community. It was stoked up and all the women who had prepared their dough lined up awaiting their turn. We were cordially invited but were last in the pecking order, so we baked late into the night. Each family had erected a shrine in their house, crowded with this bread and other holiday foods, beverages and bright orange and yellow marigolds sold in the markets for the occasion.

Barbara was included on a trek with Juan's family up river to the children's graveyard to bury and mourn one of the many deceased babies of the community. She had painted designs on wooden crosses for the procession. As they carried these up the tributary to the site, plenty of mezcal was passed around in the traditional recycled Fanta (soft drink) bottles. They buried the child and had a boozy picnic before returning to the village.

It is customary to dance and party on top of the graves as a way to keep the memories, and therefore the spirits, of the ancestors alive. Although incorporated by the Catholic Church as All Souls' Day, this ceremony is adapted from ancient civilizations' wisdom cultures. They seem to me a much healthier attitude toward the natural order of life and death than the puritanical silence around death we espouse in North America, and I have carried this forward into my present, decades after living with the Zapotec Indian people of Mexico.

I noticed that sweet Adela from the *tienda* was making terracotta bowls and asked where she got the clay. She led me to a spot in the jungle where she scooped out the sticky reddish mud. Still carrying a small plastic chess set in my gear, I decided to create a clay set. At one point I had a job painting the Mexican Army logo on the side of a new truck, and one of the officers came to my hut for a chess game. He left in an angry huff of machismo when I won the match. Score no points for a liberated woman in Mexico!

Barbara and I had also been hired to paint the inside of the high-ceilinged rooms at a Puerto Escondido motel with brightly colored tempera (sky blue, bright salmon, lime green), a strenuous and rather boring job. While we took a lunch break on a bench outside the motel, an immigration officer sat down to interview us. We managed to act like guests instead of the "illegal" workers we were! By then we had lived here for the allotted six months and had traveled again to Guatemala to renew our visas. This time we had been given only three more months.

We had more adventures on that second round trip to the southern border but no longer needed a guide. When we stopped in Oaxaca City on the return, I was wearing the original jeans I had brought from Canada. Some lady vendors of *huipils,* (embroidered blouses), singled me out as *feia,* or ugly, because it had not yet been accepted for women to wear pants, and it happened that both Barbara and Serena were wearing dresses that day. The comment stung as I was usually considered pretty, part of my normal identity.

We met an expatriated gay black American man named Wendell, who let us stay at his apartment. He was arrested one night for dancing naked in the fountain in the main *zocalo*, or square. He was fond of saying that he "did not 'moon', but 'eclipse.'" He generally behaved scandalously and was immensely entertaining. We noticed that when the daily Oaxaca vegetable market shut down for the evening, there were loads of bruised or slightly wilted produce left behind. We scooped it up and made lovely meals in Wendell's kitchen.

Back at the village, Barb came down with a high, jaw-shivering fever. Juan's mother Maria Luisa cared for her like a daughter, nursing her through the symptoms she recognized as malaria. Barbara acknowledged that good care and how it was responsible for her survival of the severe disease. Henceforth she kept a supply of *Quinina* from the *farmacia* in town to control the symptoms when they recurred.

Later, Serena also came down with a fever and I feared it might be the mosquito-borne malaria. Again I remembered the ominous words of the palm reader and asked the villagers about a doctor. I was directed to the local medicine woman, Licha, whom they called *bruja,* or witch. I carried my sweating daughter to a shack on the outskirts of the village, near the sesame fields. I never discovered her history, but the craggy-skinned Licha had a grown daughter and now lived alone, which was unique in the village of multi-generational family compounds. She stoked up her fire and confidently threw a handful of whole leaves into boiling water. She had Serena drink the brew and gave me the rest to take away with us. The nature of the leaves remains a mystery, but to my relief Serena revived almost immediately, the fever gone — not malaria.

With this subsistence lifestyle there was the daily supply of *lena,* dry reeds and kindling, to collect for cooking our tortillas, rice and beans, fish, or vegetable *caldo* (soup). There was the prolific edible ground cover weed *verdolaga* (purslane) we picked and used as greens. Occasionally we made an "omelet" with turtle eggs. We followed Juan and the village boys along the obscure trail through the jungle to the beach when the turtles were nesting in the sand. The eggs looked like dented ping-pong balls and the contents had a grainy texture but added to our nutrition. At certain tides there was a run of miniature shrimp up the river and we learned how to harvest them with a strainer for protein and flavoring. We learned that mezcal was used to disinfect everything, from knives to flesh wounds.

I sketched many of the scenes and sent them home in letters and kept a small journal as well. Settled back in the village we became complacent; after the three months passed, we did not find the energy or the will to travel again but just continued our lives there. We had occasional news of family events; my brother married a college sweetheart, and my mother's sister died suddenly of a heart attack at age fifty. These events seemed remote from our day-to-day routines, and Barbara had become the de facto daughter-in-law to Juan's family.

Abrupt Departure

"All changes, even the most longed for, have their melancholy, for what we leave behind us is a part of ourselves; we must die to one life before we can enter another."
Anatole France

A short distance up the highway lived Gorge, a mid-twenties Hispanic American from L.A., with his blond American lover Marcus, who reminded me of the starry-eyed scarecrow from *The Wizard of Oz*. We often saw them on our way to town, and one day Gorge asked to borrow my horse for an errand. I agreed and thought no more of it. At that same time the big news on the village "grapevine" was that Miguel-Angel had been hurt in a motorcycle accident and was recuperating at his house where we had first been guests. I concocted a garlic and zucchini *caldo* in my large pot, caught Golondrina, and rode up the trail bareback, balancing the pot under one arm. I found him alone, badly bruised with skin burns but able to walk. He was quite surprised to see me and grateful for the neighborly gesture.

The very next afternoon, that friendly immigration officer we had met in town appeared at the *tienda*, asking for us "girls." He called us to his truck and asked if we had a horse. It came out that Gorge had ridden Golondrina to town with a pouch of fresh marijuana to sell to the hippies on the beach. The officer said he knew we were "good girls," not involved with drugs, but he then asked to see our passports. We knew they were expired and held our breaths as he declared *No hay papeles,* which gave him no choice but to take us away. Many residents had gathered around to watch this scene, and some of them cried as we gathered our few belongings, especially Juan's mother. I bequeathed the animals to Adela who had always been so tenderly kind to all of us. We too shed tears, feeling as though we had become truly part of their interdependent village fabric, and we were being ripped out without warning.

I am ever grateful for that rare taste of life which no longer exists today. In 2018 Barbara sent a YouTube link to a webcam tour of La Barra. Riding his bicycle through the streets, a boy passed colorful cement block houses which appeared to have indoor plumbing, televisions, even washing machines. Apparently surfers had discovered attractive big waves and brought wealth and progress to the enclave.

In 1974 there had been only a dirt trail through the jungle, dense foliage sprinkled with banana and papaya trees, to that all but inaccessible beach. Now there is a cafe/bar and an unfinished, abandoned structure several stories high, perhaps an overambitious plan for a resort. There is not a trace of the simple, more primitive life we knew more than forty years past.

Our deportation began in the back of the pickup truck confiscated from Gorge. Crowded together with us three were also Gorge, Marcus and their large German Shepherd. We stopped for an overnight in a jail in Acapulco where we were put in a holding cell with a bright bare light bulb. They did bring in a cot for Serena, but I had a strong headache from the fumes of the truck and could not sleep on the floor. There were stale tortillas stuck in the high window grates which had been nibbled by cockroaches to resemble lace doilies.

Periodically, loud ladies of the night, who presumably had not "paid their dues," were thrown in with us, protesting and banging on the bars. In the morning we were marched through the hall between the permanent cells. The occupants had creatively draped fabric around their bunks for privacy and we heard that these women did much of the embroidery sold in the tourist markets. Breakfast in the cafeteria consisted of a thin gruel and weak tin-tasting coffee. The boys reported an even more difficult night in the men's side where the inmates threatened to murder the dog.

We were loaded into the truck and driven to Mexico City. It sprawls at 7,500 feet above sea level and was very cold that February (it snowed for the first time in twelve years).

The Detention Center was unheated and we had only the light clothing needed for the tropics of southern Mexico. Magic Barbara produced a worn paperback copy of *The Hobbit* which we took turns reading aloud while huddling together in a bunk for warmth, Serena sandwiched between us. This helped to pass the hours and days, reading about the strange adventures of Middle Earth, even as we were experiencing our own rather surreal adventure awaiting news of our destiny. After a week or so we were ushered into the office of *El Hefe,* The Boss, where the agents seemed befuddled. Serena and I had American passports and could therefore be escorted to the U.S. border. However, Barbara's plight was less clear. The U.S. would not accept a British citizen, and she had long since cashed in her return plane ticket to England, so her fate was undetermined.

Soon all of us Americans were unceremoniously put back in the truck and dropped off in El Paso, western Texas. I began hitchhiking with Serena, heading for home in Northern California. After a few shorter rides, we were picked up by a woman on her way to L.A. who wanted company. She liked us and loaned us enough money to take the bus from L.A. to San Francisco where we showed up safely on "Grandma's doorstep."

Barbara was still awaiting her fate alone in Mexico City. The authorities at last determined that as a "crown subject" she would be accepted in Belize, formerly British Honduras, part of the Yucatan Peninsula, adjoining Guatemala at the southeastern tip of Mexico. There she became involved with a beautiful Creole artist specializing in sign painting. They lived together, she became pregnant and they married. Barbara helped him with signs and a tee shirt printing business and learned the colorful creole "pidgin" vernacular.

Her husband was also a notorious gambler and she often had to track him down on payday to retrieve enough money to cover rent and electricity. Baby Jonny was born and when the father landed in jail, Barbara took the baby to stay with a friend in New Hampshire and then went back to England. For a few years she worried that the father would pursue them and try to reclaim his son, but apparently he had been incarcerated for years and nothing was ever heard from him directly.

Re-entry

We lived with my parents for several months, with Serena, now seven, enrolled in a nearby school. I caught up with the American friends we had met in Baja. One of the members of the group renting the villa in La Paz had a house-painting company. I made an excellent wage painting the fine detail trim on French windows, doors and moldings. This same fellow turned over to me his job of lay-out artist for *Argosy*, the archery magazine. When my family had gone through their dedicated phase of archery my father had subscribed to that periodical, so I knew it well. However none of these activities, though gainful employment, were satisfying my creative drive as an artist.

The larger group of friends welcomed me as they frequently gathered at the No Name Bar in Sausalito. I became enamored with another of their cohorts, photographer Lazlo. He invited me to his apartment in San Francisco near Mission Dolores for his favorite beverage, Stolichnaya (Russian vodka) and to photograph me. He led me down the street to a graffiti wall painted with a huge orange question mark where I briefly shed my coat for an enigmatic nude shot on the sidewalk.

We backpacked with another couple to a wilderness area lake where he posed me curled on a wooden raft in the early morning mist. When my painting contractor boss asked me to marry him, declaring he would be happy to take care of me and Serena, I had to refuse. My heartstrings were being pulled by Lazlo, who actually had another faithful girl-friend waiting for our passionate fling to end. It did, but we remained lifelong friends.

The book that then caught my attention was *Grist for the Mill* by psychologist Richard Alpert who found a guru in India and had been renamed Ram Dass, or Servant of God. It was a guide to any westerner on the path to becoming a yogi. I had read his earlier *Be Here Now,* which was later described as the "counterculture bible" and which contained a collection of aphorisms from many spiritual teachers (e.g., "Early in the journey you wonder how long the journey will take and if you will make it in this lifetime. Later you will see that where you are going is HERE and you will arrive NOW...so you stop asking.") It absolutely validated the very much "present moment" life I had long since adopted.

Another quote related to the raising of children: "Oh! I'm going to do good things for my child. Balony! That's all ego. Just work on yourself...every time you work on yourself you get calmer you hear more you sense more you are more you're more present. What are you offering a child? Not a set of social rules passing in the night...you're offering a child here and now-ness, the treasure of consciousness...the treasure of awareness." And Serena was also offering all that to me!

I especially liked the idea that the Buddha could be found in anyone, for instance a bus driver: "You will know him because the simple dance that may transpire between you — such as handing him change as you board the bus — will strengthen in you the faith in the divinity of man. It's as simple as that." I had often experienced that unifying and joyful recognition in the eyes of a stranger — with many of the village folk in Mexico, even with some of the homeless people I had passed on my way to my old job in downtown San Francisco (1969), whom I have never forgotten. This new book reinforced my faith in the spiritual journey and the flashes of "Awakening to Oneness."

During this period my generous mother was providing ballet lessons for Serena. While waiting for her, I took a jazz dance class in the same building and observed for the first time a belly dance class taught by the famous Bert Balladine. I watched transfixed as the women hip-bumped, undulated and twirled around the circle, looking so filled with joy. I wanted to perform, but the jazz teacher told me I was "not quite performance material." So when summer of 1975 arrived, I suggested I take Serena to live at the family mountain cabin to continue the barefoot, close-to-nature lifestyle we had enjoyed in Mexico. My parents' weekends were now absorbed by their hobby, bay sailing, so the Dorrington cabin sat vacant and they agreed we could move in temporarily.

Dorrington History

"Look deep into nature and then you will understand every-thing better." Albert Einstein

We relocated to Dorrington, just off Highway 4 on Ebbetts Pass, where I had a rich family history growing up. While camping in the late 1950s at Calaveras Big Trees State Park, it had started snowing heavily. Looking for more substantial lodging, we stopped at the Historic Dorrington Hotel (built in 1852), which also had available rental cabins at the edge of a large picturesque meadow situated at 4,700 feet above sea level. Captivated by the area, my father asked to be notified if any of the small dwellings surrounding the meadow should come up for sale. The one to become our second home was situated across the meadow, just across a clear stream, and down a dusty dirt road a quarter of a mile off the main highway (not navigable by vehicle in winter).

The one-room structure held nothing more than a large wood stove for cooking and heat. There was an outhouse, or "biffy," up the hill in the forest behind. Being head of that steadfastly "do-it-yourself" family, my father creatively transformed the space to accommodate our family of five by partitioning a bar area for the "kitchen," one corner walled off containing three tiers of bunk beds for the kids, and a sofa-bed for the parents. The "living room" was the great outdoors. They hired a well-digger and years later added a wing with actual plumbing and an attic for slumber parties with friends and cousins. In winter our supplies were piled onto a toboggan and we snowshoed down the lane, often with me pulling, serving as the family pack horse. I loved the physicality and feeling the workout in my legs (as a dancer, I still do). I learned to ski (holding a library book with instructions), and we spent happy summers exploring the creek and swimming at the local public pool across from the old hotel.

The owners of all that Dorrington property, including the meadow acreage, built a new house and several new A-frame rental cabins near the pool and became family friends.

Another insurance family from Marin also had their second home across the highway and our family visited with their four boys who invited us to share their ski tow, small pool, and summer stables (there was a companion of a similar age for each of us, my middle sister, younger brother, and a romantic interest for me).

During those teen years, spending nearly every weekend and most of the summers at Dorrington took its toll on my social life at school. On the other hand, time spent in the mountains brought us intimately close to the wonders of nature. On a hillside down the creek, I remember having a particularly religious experience lying on the grass watching clouds whisk across the sky. It seemed to me I suddenly understood God and the oneness of us all. I also transferred my daydreams of being a heroine among boys to the mountain community. I knitted my own ski sweater and made my own first hot pink bikini with those fantasies roiling in my head. Within walking distance of the Dorrington pool was a vacation cabin subdivision, Snowshoe Springs, with its own lake, evening dances, and plenty of kids of all ages we frequently met at the pool.

The Water Show

"Reach for the stars with your toes." Unknown

Early in life I was deathly afraid of water and at the age
of eight, my first swimming lessons were an ordeal for all
concerned. Thanks to persistent teachers, after a few seasons
I became fluent with all the strokes, even diving off the high
board, enjoying the rivers and lakes at family campsites,
and taking synchronized swimming classes at the YWCA.
Esther Williams films from Hollywood glamorized water
ballet and fascinated me. I had year after year admired the
lifeguards at the Dorrington pool so was inspired to add
an evening lifeguard training course to my high school
curriculum. After graduation I asked for the summer job
of lifeguard at the Dorrington pool, which was divided
between me and a local girl who needed the work.

We were housed in the apartment attached to the owners'
home so as to be properly chaperoned in our parents'
absence. I split my time between the pool and tending a
horse that my rancher uncle had given me, kept in a corral
at the cabin at the other end of the meadow. Every year on
closing the pool at the Labor Day weekend holiday, it was a
tradition for the pool to host a gala Water Show. The main
attraction was a local man who performed an expert clown
trick diving act.

This year (1964) I procured a budget from Andy & Flo, the owners, for music and costume materials and set about choreographing other numbers for the show, which I called "World Fair." Two of the local girls my age and I formed the "trio of stars" while I organized the rest of the pool regulars to open the show, floating on their backs holding candles in formations around the pool. I used Martin Denny's instrumental "Quiet Village" interspersed with bird calls for a tropical number, our bikinis bedecked with silk flowers.

Another piece featured three cowboys carrying us out of the dressing room and tossing us into the pool. We were dressed as saloon girls with colorful tulle headdresses and bustles as we extended our pointed toes and did a watery can-can to Offenbach's famous music. Not bad for a seventeen-year-old with her only experience being home productions for parents of the neighborhood.

After so much excited preparation, the whole show came close to not happening at all. The owner Andy caught me canoodling at the cabin with a boy I knew in high school who followed me to the mountains. Andy wanted to fire me on the spot and cancel the show. He was worried that I would turn up pregnant and my parents would never forgive him. It took a lot to convince him I was still a virgin Catholic girl. When he asked "What? Are you not human?" I tearfully pleaded he could "have me checked." On the condition that I never see that boy again, he allowed me to keep the job and the show went on. And spoiler alert — it held the seeds of many of my future endeavors, combining my then embryonic skills as theatrical costumer, dancer, choreographer and show producer.

In spite of this success, I went off to college harboring a bundle of social insecurities with no definite goal in mind, save a vague notion of becoming a teacher. My sister later commented (acidly) that "our parents only raised us to be housewives and nature girls."

I also thank them for imparting such a strong sense of self-reliance, adaptability and creativity which carried me through life's surprising twists. It may not have been their intent to prepare me so well for the path I followed — that of a free spirit! In fact my father later lamented that they had been too much the "task masters" with me, the eldest of the three, and to that he attributed my complete rebellion. Perhaps, but in truth the entire Baby Boomer generation was united in this zeitgeist of freedom and experimentation.

It seems that after the constant emphasis on social propriety ("good girl") and education, we all craved reconnection to a more primitive, instinctual, natural and honest life, soon to be personified by the hippie movement.

The Dorrington Animals

*"Forget not that the earth delights to feel your bare feet
and the winds long to play with your hair."*
Khalil Gibran

When I returned in 1975 at the age of twenty-eight, the face of
Dorrington had changed with the addition of a grocery store
and gas station, and the pool filled in to support a real estate
office. But the meadow and national forest remained pristine;
the fragrant sugar pines, creek flora sprouting from its time-
less boulders, the dusty road to the cabin — all felt familiar
and welcoming.

We settled in with no car or TV and a young St. Bernard my
mother had bred and given to Serena. I found a couple of
sign-painting jobs and started hanging out with the group of
twenty-something locals who congregated around the pool
table and danced to the jukebox at the nearby Camp Connell
Bar & Grill. There was an equal mix of irreverent rednecks,
hippies and artists. I became known as Camp Connell D, a
kind of wild woman party girl, tan and strong, occasionally
entertaining the gang by doing yoga on the bar.

A whole group of us often went skinny-dipping in the
Stanislaus River and acted generally rowdy, earning the moni-
ker "Dorrington Animals," which referred to a bird-like sound
we used to communicate with each other across the meadow.

By fall we had moved out of the cabin and in with one of the locals along the highway, which made it much easier for Serena to catch the school bus to Arnold, seven miles down the mountain. I worked cleaning the greasy commercial grill and other rental cabins around Camp Connell and Dorrington. We harvested apples from an abandoned orchard and I baked a lot of pies. I'm sure my parents wondered what I was doing when they came to celebrate Serena's eighth birthday with a party at the cabin that fall.

Unity Arts

"If you do not change direction, you may end up in the direction you are heading." Lao Tzu

I was approached that fall (still 1975) by a fellow with a solo carved-wood sign business who was impressed by one of the prominently displayed painted signs I had done. He needed help on a new commission, to be hand-painted for the same realtor. He shared a well-tooled workshop with a dulcimer maker in an old apple barn and put me to work there.

Smitty was divorced and shared custody of his five-year-old daughter Justine. He drove a restored Model A flatbed truck with an artistically carved-wood sign advertising his company, Unity Arts. After a few weeks working together, it became obvious that we should join forces. I had recently gone off the pill and found myself pregnant from a casual "Dorrington Animal" fling.

Smit offered to drive me to the hospital for an abortion and tubal ligation, recommended by a disapproving doctor to prevent further pregnancies. I agreed, thinking that raising one child as a single mother was enough and I would never wish for more. Smit was there when I awoke from the anesthesia and gave me the sweetest, most memorable kiss.

I thought all men should be that sensitive and loving. And I joyfully welcomed his little daughter into our lives.

Smit and I found a farmhouse for rent with a large garage lower down the mountain. We moved the business there and produced some beautiful work around the county. I was repainting the interior of the house when Mom and Dad stopped by on their way to the cabin to see us. Smitty was the first boyfriend of mine they actually liked. They seemed to bond over the Model A truck, which Smit immaculately maintained. My father had recently been diagnosed with melanoma, but we had no idea how serious the prognosis was. Mom told me he had had a growth removed from his back, and I remember murmuring some platitude like "I hope you get well soon" from the top of a ladder with no inkling that my father might be terminally ill. We conducted business that fall and winter in the foothills, though for me there occurred one grandly serendipitous discovery.

We attended large crafts fairs, showing our portfolio from a corner of our friend's ceramics booth and selling to other vendors who wished to upgrade their booth signage. The 1975 Harvest Festival was a major happening with live bands and after-parties for the artists. As I danced my wild sinuous freestyle, a friend dubbed me "Slither" and invited me to a dance class she was sure I would like. This was my first Belly Dance experience, and my body, mind, and soul rejoiced. This was a momentous gift which forever transformed and enhanced my life!

Model A Flatbed in the Sierras 1976. Bufano, Smit, D, Justine, Serena

Serena, age 8, Justine, age 5

Unity Arts Sign, Arnold, CA 1977

Carved Unity Arts Sign, Placerville, CA 1977

The Dance of Life

"Your inner Belly Dancer...is your inner sensuality, your highest femininity, your great esteemed self made more apparent." Leandra J. Kalsy

From the first moment, this new world of dance felt natural and right. The feminine movements had names like "Moon Circle," "Figure 8," or "Maya," and could be perfected. With practice we all learned to isolate each part of the body yet retain our own individuality in the execution. This was truly a dance of Women's Liberation, a way to legitimately express our sensuality and proudly shine our light! And it was a full-body workout, increasing our strength and flexibility in a graceful way to beautiful music and rousing intricate drum rhythms. This "most ancient woman's dance" activated all the energy centers (Chakras), connected us to our life source (belly), and channeled our tendencies towards wildness. I felt accepted by all the girls and women in the class, and for the first time felt a bonding and excitement during every class.

I had previously been captivated by belly dancers on stage at the Calaveras Jumping Frog Fair and secretly wished to be there with them, so I practiced every spare moment. Our teacher in Murphys was the sister of the woman who directed that troupe at the fair (Asia Killeen). I was so diligent and enthusiastic I was taken to her for private lessons in Stockton and was given the sword balancing solo dance the following year on that same stage. It was such a high moment as I emerged from the tent and spun onto the stage when the drumming began, nervous and excited, carrying the sword overhead in both hands. After contrasting some sinuous undulations with the shaft of unyielding metal, I slowly and suspensefully placed the sword at the center point on the top of my head. Then, as depicted in 18th century engravings of Egyptian dancers, I continued swaying, hip popping and spinning, keeping the sword aloft, proud to demonstrate the playful use a woman makes of a potentially dangerous weapon.

At one of the craft fairs Unity Arts was contracted to do a half-dozen all-painted advertising signs, my specialty, for a motorcycle race track down in Woodland near Sacramento. It was spring break from school. Smit decided to take the week surfing with a pal and dropped Serena off to spend the vacation with my parents in the Bay Area while I stayed to paint the large signs (each was a full four-foot by eight-foot sheet of plywood).

Serena was looking forward to time with her doting grandparents. Smit's five-year-old daughter Justine had been staying with us in Serena's room and though the girls played well together, sharing me was a difficult adjustment for Serena. Used to being an only child, she felt competitive. There had been a few scenes and I had to take care not to show undue affection to Justine. They were both budding artists and I was careful to give equal praise to their lovely drawings.

As Serena got into the car with Smit, I remember saying "I love you — and please do everything Grandma and Grandpa say." I had no doubt she would, as they cherished her and she enjoyed being with them. She would be returning to the mountains with my parents for the large family Easter weekend gathering in Dorrington in April 1976.

At the end of the week Smit and I loaded the fresh signs into the back of the Model A truck and chugged our way through the foothills at its maximum speed of thirty-five miles per hour. We arrived in time for the signs to be installed around the "crashboard" of the racetrack. The man in charge invited us to dine with his family, then be his guests to watch his teenage son compete in the race.

Crash

"When you are sorrowful, look again in your heart, and you shall see that in truth you are weeping for that which has been your delight." Kahlil Gibran

We were in high spirits after dinner and several margaritas as we settled into the bleachers. Around 10 pm as we cheered for our hosts' son, there was a crash. The boy was pulled from beneath the flipped-over machine as we rushed down to the track. I felt a strong empathetic rush of adrenaline and fear beside his mother, dreading the worst. Then I joined in her relief to see the boy was dazed and bruised but alive and well.

After spending the night at their home, we were taken in the morning to collect our paycheck at the office, a contractor's shed equipped with a desk and phone. We found a message from Smit's ex-wife asking me to call her immediately. Smit had given her this contact number in case of emergency (no cell phones). I put through the call to Jane who lived in Sonora. She said, "There's been an accident," then... silence. In that few seconds my mind ran through a gamut of hideous scenarios. I took in a huge breath and finally asked "Yes — who's missing?" Slowly came the answer "Your Dad...and Serena." It had happened at 10 pm the night before, the same time as the motorcycle mishap.

That breath exhaled in a long, wailing "No-o-o-o-o-o-o" which seemed to come up from out of the earth through my feet and whole body. Then a tumble of questions: "Are you *sure*? Maybe you don't really know since you live across the river in Sonora? Maybe they are just in the hospital?" As she explained that the only survivor was my mother, who *was* in the San Andreas County Hospital, I could listen no more and handed the phone off to Smit.

I stepped outside to try to breathe. The April morning colors were intensified, jewel tone viridian greens, pure azure sky. Gazing upward I perceived two distinct vertical columns of sparkly golden light, side by side, one slightly higher, and I very clearly heard this message: "We're okay, we're okay. Go take care of Mom." That miraculous vision, or spiritual communication, did help ground me for the disorienting days ahead.

In the interest of speed, we borrowed a spare vehicle, faster than the pokey Model A. It was an older VW double cab pickup truck, which belched blue smoke from the exhaust pipe. During that ride, Smit, with his usual forward think-ing, said to me, "Do you realize you are now free to go dance around the world?" I found myself in a completely altered state, going from being a Mom to suddenly not. In that raw moment, still unaware of the tsunami of grief to come, the seed was planted. The notion of dancing around the world took years to germinate but eventually did come to pass. In retrospect that prophecy showed how well Smit understood my essence, the gypsy soul dancer, hungry for travel and adventure. I believe he was attempting to show me a silver lining full of potential future possibilities.

As might be expected, the next months were difficult; I clung to our relationship, our business, and most of all to the dance, as if to a lifeline in a stormy sea of emotions. Years later I studied the "mechanics" of grief in depth, to become a Heartbreak to Happiness Certified Grief Coach. Our narrow culture typically does not equate loss with growth and evolution. It is more common to want to get through the grief and get back to normal. But in truth we can never "go back" to the same routines or identity we had considered immutable. Deep grief offers us an opportunity to choose to learn, grow, develop our gifts, and find new ways to share them.

When we did reach the foothills near San Andreas, we passed the historic pioneer cemetery — very near where the accident had occurred. We were stopped by the highway patrol, issuing us a ticket for the polluting exhaust. Then, learning of the situation, they gave us an escort the rest of the way to the hospital. Many of my relatives who had also been on their way to our Easter feast were scattered in crying clusters on the front lawn.

I hurried in and found Mom lying in bed in a darkened room, literally trying to die. Her first words to me were "I killed them." Mine to her were "No, Mom, another hand was on that wheel beside your own." Later she related being revived by my "hot, Anna Magnani breath," recalling an intense Italian actress revered by our Italian family (she won a 1955 Oscar for *The Rose Tattoo* with Burt Lancaster).

The details of the accident were slowly pieced together, though Mom could never explain why the car had swerved and rolled over. To me this further corroborated that the whole thing was "meant to be." The Jeep Wagoneer had a plastic roof, which popped off the metal body with the torque of the twisting car. Mom's driver's seatbelt broke and she was found passed out on the road from "a bump on the head." Serena had been sleeping in the back seat and was thrown with some force onto the pavement, and my father had been held by his seatbelt while the roof came down, slicing into his neck and very probably saving him a long and painful demise from his melanoma.

I had the irrepressible urge to see Serena, feeling that, as I had given birth, I must close the loop and see her in death.

My sister and brother accompanied me to the small funeral home run by the county coroner. He looked startled when I asked to see my daughter's body, saying "Okay, but you don't want to see your father until after the makeup." Apparently my well-intentioned uncle had made arrangements for them to be shipped and prepared for a regular funeral in the Bay Area. I declared they were to be cremated according to my mother's wishes.

We waited a long time before Serena was wheeled out on a gurney. Her hair had been freshly washed and fanned out onto the pillow. She looked positively angelic with a bloodless gash on one cheek and appeared to be peacefully sleeping. As my siblings wept quietly beside us, I thanked her for accompanying me through such a full life of eight-and-a-half years and kissed her cheek one last time, now "cold as the clay."

Responding to my questioning, the coroner assured me that she went directly from sleep to death, and did not suffer. He also informed us that it was too late to change the order for the bodies to be transported, so we would have to pay the extra fees. Mom was released from the hospital and moved to a local motel where the family holed up for a couple of mournful days. She divulged that Dad's illness had progressed and they had conversations about sailing the boat out onto the ocean where they would sink with it together. She kept wondering why Serena got to go with him instead of her, his wife of thirty years. She said the time had gone by in a blink. Yet it was comforting to think their souls left this plane together with Serena in her role as "angel."

Smit and I packed some tools and moved into the San Rafael house with Mom for a few months. Though I had gained some immediate spiritual acceptance from that miraculous vision, I had yet to weather the human agony of the loss of my child. During that time, I consulted a doctor about severe chest pains. He confirmed that I was not having a heart attack and said they were caused by "just grief." I am now thankful that he did not prescribe any sedatives as is commonly done today. These may take the edge off the anxiety, but in my experience only prolong the suffering. We are wired to withstand the onslaught of intense grief, and we need to feel the depth of the varied emotions before we can truly release them.

Not surprisingly, my mother cried continuously as we made arrangements for a memorial. She took Serena's ballet slippers to be copper-plated and we each kept one. We invited the family to gather on the slope of Mount Tamalpais where my parents had done much of their courting just after my father returned from the war (WW2). Mom had gotten me a maxi-dress from Betsey Johnson, covered with a profusion of small multicolored flowers and butterflies in honor of Serena's taste. I had composed a poem to read, including a few quotes from Kahlil Gibran's tract that seemed so clear to me now — "Your children are not your children."

People spoke highly of my wonderful father while an ephemeral butterfly persistently fluttered around us. Afterwards we took the two white cardboard cartons of ashes onto the family sailboat, accompanied by a neighbor's twin boat alongside, out under the Golden Gate Bridge. As we released the ashes, two white gulls swooped between the two vessels. It seemed their souls were there with us, to help ease the final farewell.

Transition

"As long as I can I will look at this world for both of us. As long as I can I will laugh with the birds, I will sing with the flowers, I will pray to the stars, for both of us." Sascha

Smit and I kept Mom company hoping to console her through her momentous grief. As for me, I found that moving my body through dance and working my art helped to ease my own grief. Smit and I found some logo and sign design work, and I sought out every available belly dance teacher in the Bay Area.

My finger cymbal technique was still rudimentary, so I signed up for private classes and workshops and dropped in to the major studios established in San Francisco. These valuable "cross-pollination" experiences expanded my skills and gave me a window into the belly dance scene. Smit used one of his powerful drills to punch holes in some Mid-Eastern coins and I assembled my first jingly coin belt and bra set.

The plan emerged for us to move back to the Dorrington cabin to help supervise the building of a large barn on the land across the creek. Mom helped design the barn interior as a clever art studio with living space and hired Smit's contractor friend, Dave, who moved in with us for the duration of the job. "The Accident," as it came to be known, had multiple impacts on our family.

My brother was trying to emulate Dad by working a high-profile office job, recruiting student engineers for Cogswell College in San Francisco. This included travel to Asia, many three-martini lunches, and increasing mountains of cocaine. He found one of our jobs for us there at the campus — painting a stylized mural of cogs and gears inside the school rotunda.

My sister was simply at loose ends, working dead-end retail jobs. She claimed she had been "fired from college" by our parents who disapproved of her live-in boyfriend in Berkeley. She decided to join us at the cabin and used her baking talents to produce deserts for several mountain restaurants. She and Dave spent hours together playing guitars, inevitably becoming lovers, and later marrying.

Some sleepless nights I would slip out of the cabin to make my way down the creek-side trail by moonlight. I would find myself first crying, which naturally led to wailing, then howling. This felt like the only way to "massage" my heart — with unearthly sounds emanating from the depths of the pain. I was lucky enough to be living in a sparsely populated area and to be able to follow my instincts without reserve.

Most often in "Western society" these sounds are considered disturbing, and we are urged to sedately suppress this authentic expression. From my intense experience, I recommend to anyone grieving to find a way to uninhibitedly wail as often as necessary as a natural healing practice. (Later in my travels I witnessed professional mourners who wail along with the family to facilitate giving voice to their grief.)

My other outlet was dance. The women had formed a troupe, and they held me in their circle with such tenderness. We rehearsed at the home of another mother whose son had a special bond with Serena. We shared cups of tea and memories. We all choreographed together as a cooperative and my sister, with her ballet background, joined in. We both mastered the balancing of a sword and other objects on our heads while doing graceful floorwork and backbends, advancing to "Turkish Drops" and "Berber Knee Walks," the more athletic side of belly dance.

It was during this time that I was invited to dance at the big fair, fulfilling the dream. Our troupe created many more performance opportunities with Smit accompanying us on his dulcimer, providing the exotic music in "Aeolian Tuning." We all danced on the back of his Model A flatbed truck at the Arnold Fourth of July Fair and at any restaurant or bar that would have us. I taught Smit's adorable blond daughter Justine some routines so she could join us.

Most of the younger people who lived in that mountain community might have been regarded as anarchistic hippies by the older locals. There was a pervading consciousness of living off the grid, or at least on our own terms, so as to avoid the repression of human spirit, or working for The Man. Living a free life was a subtly subversive statement in itself. The book of the day was *Even Cowgirls Get the Blues* by Tom Robbins, who packed his prose with idealistic social experiments and dialectic. About the problem of "freedom" he wrote:

> "No matter how much people long to be free...an aversion to freedom is right there in their DNA. For eons of evolutionary time, our DNA has been whispering into the ears of our cells that we are, each one of us, the most precious thing in the universe and that any action that entails the slightest risk may have consequences of universal importance...Conversely, the yearning for freedom, the risky belief that there is nothing to lose and nothing to gain, is also in our DNA. But it's of much more recent evolutionary origin...the desire for security, the will to survive, is of much greater antiquity...
>
> To live fully one must be free, but to be free one must give up security. How's that for paradox?

There are no group solutions! Each individual must work it out for himself. There are guides all right, but even the wisest guides are blind in your section of the burrow. No. All a person can do in this life is to gather about him his integrity, his imagination and his individuality — and with these ever with him, out front and in sharp focus — leap into a dance of experience.

Be your own master/Jesus/flying saucer. Rescue yourself. Be your own Valentine. Free the heart!"

I found him to be a wryly articulate spokesperson of the late seventies, as well as of my own Aquarian open-mindedness and idealism. We even got my mother to read that book to help her understand our youthful rationale.

The barn was built by October 1977 and we celebrated, hosting a large Halloween costume party. It was one of those uncomfortable occasions when I was unsure of how I fit in — showing me I was still searching for my new non-mother identity.

In an attempt to cheer herself up, my own mother decided to take me on a trip with her to Tahiti, where she had booked us into the Club Med resort on Moorea. At first our luggage did not arrive, so we bought ourselves new bathing suits and *pareus* (colorful cloth to wrap and drape), then discovered we did not need any other clothing.

We did a lot of morning yoga, daily snorkeling, and in the evening Tahitian dance. Everyone, women and men, wore a hibiscus blossom tucked behind one ear; the left side for "heart is won" and the right for "looking." One of the staff wore it squarely on top, proclaiming himself "undecided." I brought along my sword (thank goodness the luggage did arrive intact), in case there was a talent show.

We usually ate at the circular tables with a group of upbeat vacationers who included us in their activities. These meals always featured unlimited pitchers of sangria (fruit and wine punch) and were usually followed by siesta time in our individual *fares*, or thatched huts.

Indeed there was a talent show, and on that day the organizers called a rehearsal right after lunch. After the wine, I could not keep that sword from slipping off my head and clanging onto the tile stage. The French staff were snootily dubious and wanted to cut my act.

But by evening I surprised them all with a sober and smooth performance and had learned that alcohol was a hindrance. I also understood that a full stomach was not conducive to a crisp performance. I went on to habitually abstain from anything but water for three hours before setting foot on stage. This became a "devotional" practice which I adhere to even today. After that talent show the staff and cast gathered at the Tiki Bar for late night drinks. I ordered a virgin coconut drink since I was already so high on dance.

Arnold 4th of July Parade 1977. Troupe Salaam Alaikum, D
Sword, Sister Louise seated far right

Teaching Justine, Dorrington 1977. Justine, D

Move to Hawaii 1977. Smit.

The Big Island

"This is Pele's place and we as descendents of akua (ele-mental spirits) and descendents of the land need to live in harmony with the elements and the land. Humans are not the most important things on earth, the elements are. As long as Pele is erupting we say she is dancing."
Lilikala Kame'eleihiwa

The tropical atmosphere of Tahiti had suited me and as we had friends living in Hawaii, Smit was up for a scouting trip to visit them and check out several islands for relocation. We "felt the Aloha" and settled on the big island of Hawaii with its many microclimates and the live volcano at Mauna Kea, ruled by Madam Pele.

We shipped our little Toyota pickup filled with our major tools, sold the Model A and left the snowy mountain winter behind. It was agreed that we would take Smit's daughter, five-year-old Justine, for a year and every alternate year thereafter.

While searching for a living situation, the stay with our friends became increasingly uncomfortable. We witnessed the volatile couple, goaded by alcohol and drugs, constantly at odds. Such is the unexpected intimacy when you live with people you know only from superficial social situations. But no space opened up for us.

I danced in the midst of a large music festival with Smit accompanying me on the dulcimer. We gathered an audience and afterwards a group of *haole* (non-native Hawaiian) women enthusiastically asked, "Will you teach us?" and offered a place for classes. They also became my core group of caring friends and were instrumental in helping me continue to heal from the loss of my daughter. One of the ladies created an astrological chart for Serena and found "the hand of God" triangle pointing to the date of her death. We both cried as she showed me the aspects, apparently predestined in the stars.

Through these kind people we were introduced to The Kona Light Center where we rented one of the eight rooms of the inn, and which had a separate building with a large recreation room and communal kitchen. The owner who lived in San Francisco had big dreams for the run-down place. The current managers were a stoned-out hippie couple who fantasized about adding a stained-glass dome and other imaginary improvements while they did absolutely nothing. We were happy to have low-rent temporary digs in a beautiful place surrounded by fruit trees and tropical gardens.

We used our tools to make some repairs at the inn, and a friend of the absentee owner reported to him our constructive presence at The Kona Light Center. Soon we were installed as the new managers. It seemed Madame Pele smiled upon us after all! Smit and I refurbished all the rooms and I taught my classes in the big hall. We were then responsible for renting the rooms, booking all the activities, planting and maintaining an organic vegetable garden, and later opening two days a week for a vegan buffet. We became pescatarian, or primarily vegetarian with occasional fresh fish. Our first unforgettable island Thanksgiving we shared with a friend who roasted a succulent whole eel wrapped in banana leaves in a sand pit on the beach. I completely stopped casually accepting the ubiquitous passed joints, finding the "Maui Wowie" and "Kona Gold" too strong for normal functioning, not to mention keeping all the bookings, rentals, and accounting straight!

Booking every type of workshop, we presented every type of guru, offering nearly every path to enlightenment. There were ample seekers, "Rajneeshers," Seiks, and meditators, to fill the hall continuously. Smit and I enjoyed the Seiks' Kundalini Yoga classes and adopted their habit of a 5 a.m. cold shower to start the day in white clothing for a three-part meditation including yoga poses, yogic breathing ("breath of fire"), and chanting ("Sat Nam, Hari Nam, Sat Nam Hari"). Smit commented this was good for breaking patterns, and we even attended a grueling retreat at their center on Oahu with Yogi Bhajan himself. One of his favorite quotes is, "When you don't go within, you go without."

We found a lovely hula teacher who taught a group of us for a couple of years, bringing us *haoles* up to rudimentary performance level. She always said my hips had a Middle Eastern accent. We also attracted a Russian ballet mistress, with whom I studied for the discipline of improved dance posture and crisp turns to add to my belly dance practice. I learned the classic *Sevillanas* in Flamenco class, and basic *Bharatanatyam*, the ancient classical dance of India. Another dancer led a morning jazzercise class to the thrumming disco sounds of Donna Summer ("She works hard for the money....").

Throughout it all, Smit and I had space enough on the property to produce beautifully carved signs for island businesses. In fact there was a local sign ordinance in Kona dictating that all signs be made of natural materials, so we had a built-in clientele. We explored the island, enjoyed beach time, and did experience some of Madame Pele's volcanic activity with the ash and gasses that pervade the entire island after an eruption.

There was the ubiquitous (for these times, 1977-80) women's group. We met once a week on someone's lanai *mauka* (up the mountain). One of our members was an "older" woman, perhaps fifty-ish, who seemed especially wise. She often spoke of how spiritually bankrupt was American society and its leaders. We in Hawaii were surrounded by rich spiritual tradition and it permeated our every activity, from dancing to snorkeling to doing business.

Certainly our relationships with the locals were reverent, but also with each of the stray folks who arrived to rent rooms at the Kona Light Center Inn. They had names like "Maple," "Autumn," "Love 22," and "Harmony Sprout." One single father brought his autistic son who loved to hang out during the belly dance classes and whirl to the music.

I fell "in love" with some of them, once ending up in a late-night bath with a German punk photographer. Smit was quite tolerant and wrote me this Haiku: "Laboring beside you, I watch amazed. Exquisite workmanship!" He also told me once at party where everyone was dancing wildly, "You don't need to try so hard — you have 'it' just standing there." I loved him and his unlimited creativity, but he adamantly expressed to a friend about me, "I would never marry her."

My original belly dance class ladies were ready to become a performing troupe, so we held rehearsals in the hall and I began making costumes from the saris brought from India by the Rajneeshers. By listening to my half-dozen belly dance vinyl albums, our musician friends learned to play our favorite pieces. By now I had developed my "double sword dance," balancing one on my head while moving the other to first one shoulder, then one hip. Rehearsals were like parties in themselves and we developed an ensemble to play for all our gigs: hotels, outdoor festivals, senior homes, theme parties.

We also used the Kona Light Center facility to create an event called Nights at the Casbah, cooking and serving a Mediterranean meal to accompany our entertainment. And we rented Captain Bob's Glass Bottom Boat at the Kona

Harbor to stage the floating "Cleopatra's Barge" dining experience. It was more difficult to keep our choreography together on the rocking deck, but we pulled it off!

I hosted workshops with visiting teachers, such as Hadia from Canada. Smit was learning to fly small planes and ferried us dancers to other islands for their workshops and events (Aziz of Utah taught on Kauai). I subscribed to the two belly dance periodicals of the time: *Habibi* from the West Coast, and *Arabesque*, which covered all the Eastern U.S. happenings. I poured over every article, photo and ad. There were reports from dancers who traveled to Middle Eastern countries to study the varied regional dance styles.

It seemed we were all enrolled in a massive cultural study course to learn about rhythms, history, customs, and languages to enhance our understanding of this beloved dance. A few lucky dancers had made the pilgrimage and brought back first-hand knowledge to the growing number of U.S. dancers. How I longed to be one of those pilgrims! I had always been bewitched by others' travel stories and thought now that my future travel would have a purpose — to go study the dance in its indigenous form — perhaps in Egypt itself.

Moving On

"Dance resides within us all. Some find it when joy conquers sorrow, others express it though celebration of movements; and then there are those...whose existence is dance."
Shah Asad Rizvi

After we had managed the Kona Light Center for three years, the owner came to propose a host of grandiose, impractical changes. Smit and I turned in our resignation, rented a condo near downtown Kona and a workshop space in the back of the Kona Shopping Plaza which hired us to make their main sign as well as those for the individual shops (I was happy to see some of them still intact on a return visit in 2008).

However, by mid-1980, our five-year relationship was winding down. In September Smit wrote: "Half a decade alone together, I come to you weeping, as we grow, apart. Tears of joy at last."

Our "Troupe Baladi" had been booked for several hotel shows produced by two young men fresh from Oahu. One was an up-and-coming singer-songwriter named Hunter, and the other was Robbie, a Brit who had recently broken up with his longtime girlfriend and needed a change. They played back a video of one of our performances and told me, "You don't need that troupe." Exciting feedback! I had been hoping I was ready to become a distinguished soloist and here was the confirmation I needed.

Smit made a trip to the mainland to deliver Justine to her mother while I stayed and attended a party given by these producers. I was becoming obsessed with the tall, engaging Brit, Robbie, whose gamin face echoed that of my daughter — the same wide smile and slightly slanted twinkly eyes. This resemblance was a compelling enough attraction, but he also sported long limbs and a pleasantly languid way of moving through the world. Thus he became my next big love, regaling me with tempting stories of escapades around European castles with his gang of friends.

I was also soon to discover that he was one of those rare perfect fits in the bedroom. He really got me when, while driving me to teach my class one morning, his car spluttered to a stop. He raised the hood and as I watched through the slit, his capable hands and chiseled forearms moved some spark plugs (or something) around until the car started and we arrived on time. Yes, forearms can be highly erotic! We moved into a sprawling rental house on the lava beach in Kona with his musician friend Hunter, and when the owner decided to sell it, relocated to a duplex where the upper story was rarely occupied by the owner. I was fully embroiled and trusting in this new romance and noted the Rajneesh quote: "Unless your trust has gone through many doubts it will remain impotent — from where will it gather strength and integration???"

My British friend Barbara had come to live on the island with her now four-year old son. They had stayed with me and Smit at the Kona Light Center, helping with the "restaurant" food. Then she moved to digs on a coffee plantation with other moms and kids. She did not cotton to my new British boyfriend, sneering at his jokes, and regarding him as "not quite a grown-up." My mother had come to visit and asked me what I was doing with this "drifter." Smit, who had also moved on to another girl-friend, was fine with him and even had him help in the sign shop.

Another friend of Robbie's from Glasgow stayed with us for a while. Maybe that made him homesick because Robbie began to talk about returning to London to visit his mum. I was finally ready to dance around the world and fulfill Smit's prophecy from that conversation when Serena died. My ultimate goal was to dance my way to Egypt, motherland of this dance, to study in its indigenous setting. So Robbie and I pooled our savings, totaling $6,000, and booked the first leg of our journey to stop in California to see my family.

Just after take-off on the plane Robbie divulged that his Scottish friend had stolen the TV from the upstairs unit of our last residence. I was shocked and angered while he found it funny and perfectly normal. It was dawning that I had thrown in my lot with a dishonest person. He had taken care of me after a minor operation and we both enjoyed endless games of Scrabble, so I had mistakenly deduced we held more similar values.

On the mainland my mother gave Robbie and I a first-class tour of all the best San Francisco sights including Ghirardelli Square, Fisherman's Wharf, up the Fairmont Hotel's glass elevator to its revolving cocktail lounge, The Cliff House and Seal Rock, and finally to Pasha's Turkish Restaurant to see the belly dancing. Robbie commented "They should make a movie of us," and we were spiraling upward on our romantic adventure. We talked a lot about "always," and as I wrote in my diary, he said, "I don't want to be just another statistic in your life diary." We bought a used car at a lot called "Rent a Wreck" and drove to Dorrington for a small family reunion.

After a few luxurious weeks with friends and family, we headed for Oregon to a fair I had read about in *Habibi*

Magazine, which featured belly dancing. I secured a slot in the show, plus took my first class with a teacher from Egypt. I felt like I did everything she showed us, but after class I asked her what she thought of my dancing. She replied in her charming accent, "Oh, there eez *too* much to feex!"

For the rest of the drive, Robbie and I crossed the border into Canada where they took away his U.S. residency card. We visited some friends in Vancouver, and I met a self-proclaimed grand dame of belly dance who let me dance one of her sets at the restaurant where she appeared regularly (I was encouraged by the good tips!) Then she took me under her maternal wing and gifted me with some Middle Eastern music cassettes to expand my repertoire. Traversing east across Canada, we visited acquaintances in Calgary and then continued until we reached Montreal where I had lived for several years and wanted to stop and visit old friends.

Madame Pele's Lava Flow 1979. Dhyanis Backbend
with Sword

Troupe Baladi of Kona, Hawaii, 1980. D with Sword,
Smit with Dulcimer

Barbara and Jonny (age 4), Hawaii 1980

Carved and Painted in Hawaii 1980. Dhyanis

Kona, Hawaii Children's Store
Wooden Puzzle Wall Art, 1981

Flamingos: Kona, Hawaii, Clothing Store Sign
by Dhyanis 1981

Montreal Revisited

"Because things are the way they are, things will not stay the way they are." Bertolt Brecht

At that moment in 1981, Patrick, my debilitatingly alcoholic second husband, was in the hospital, having some of his ravaged intestines removed. Miliscka, the beautiful woman who had left him in California prior to our liaison had become one of my closest allies, took me to see him. The story of those years I spent there in Quebec, between 1969 and 1973, are in an earlier chapter. Patrick was quite ill and seemed only half aware of my visit, though he did survive for several more years.

I mentioned to Miliscka that Robbie's elfin face reminded me of Serena, with whom she had been quite close. She agreed, saying "He is not to be ignored." I made a two-night guest appearance at a classy Moroccan restaurant with live music in old town Montreal and invited my friends to come and see the new me. Miliscka enthused, "She even dances with her teeth!"

Robbie's plan to save money was to dip back down to New York where he hoped to sell the car and fly an economy airline to London. At the border we were turned back, told by the guards that Robbie's visa no longer allowed him into the U.S. We were forced to spend a third of our resources on an expensive British Airways flight, which certainly annoyed me. Even so, it was exciting to be crossing over the Atlantic for my first time in early July 1981, after hearing so many tantalizing stories from abroad. Everyone smoked on planes in those days, and there were no screens, but there was pretty good food service. We passed the time playing endless games of Boggle, a more compact travel version of Scrabble using only five-letter words, and landed at last in London where I was given a three-month visa.

Taste of England

"A thin grey fog hung over the city, and the streets were very cold; for summer was in England."
Rudyard Kipling

Robbie confessed he had a low tolerance for his Mum. She lived on the outskirts of London in a complex of rented brick "council flats," with a small back garden where she "sunned" on the rare days there were any rays to be had. She worked a low-income cleaning job in a period of high unemployment; riots in working-class Brixton were being broadcast on the "tellie." In anticipation of his rare visit, his mum had put up a Welcome Home Robert sign in the front window and bought a new bed for the guestroom. She seemed to me a sweet fussbudget, as it was obvious we upset her sterile routine.

We eventually had a few heart-to-heart talks and I showed her pictures of Serena. She told me she thought Robbie had changed: "He has his head in the clouds and I cannot get through."

Everything seemed both depressed and overpriced as we wandered through the streets, popping into many betting shops, an old habit of Robbie's. We also stopped into many-a-pub and ate fish and chips wrapped in greasy newspaper. Robbie visited the taxi garage where he had previously worked to ask about a job, but there was a wait list. He also explained to me that if he did work there it would be a long-time commitment with many odd shifts, saying "It's a life." It was not one that suited him these days, after the years playing around in Hawaii.

I investigated potential dance venues at London's posh clubs and restaurants. One evening we spent hours nursing a couple of drinks at the Arabic nightspot Sheherazade where I had read that San Francisco dancer Asmahan entertained regularly. She appeared on stage only after midnight to perform an impressive half-hour set with the professional Arabic orchestra for the largely Arabic audience.

I implored the waiter to get a message to her, so afterwards she spent a few minutes at our table. She asked if I could see "Jamila Salimpour's influence" in her dance. One of the first teachers to codify the dance for Americans, Jamila presided over the largest belly dance studio in San Francisco, where I had previously dropped in, and who was the main lineage of most of my teachers. I said I could but was secretly amazed at how far she had come from the simple breakdown of steps to a true mastery of the music. She said there were no openings for dancers there, but this was my first glimpse of real night life, which starts in earnest at midnight all across Europe and the Middle East.

I managed to get an audition at a beautifully decorated Turkish restaurant, Gallipoli, in Bishop's Gate, where the owner said he liked my dancing, but he could not hire me unless I had come into the country with a special work visa. I had not foreseen this legal obstacle.

Everything in England seemed like a "Catch 22." Living with Robbie's mum was becoming claustrophobic. She graciously made dinners for us, typically overcooked and bland, and Robbie's estranged father would join us to watch television with his feet upon the coffee table, shoes off, emitting a pungent stench. His mum mentioned to me that she was surprised to see Robbie show up with a different girlfriend since she believed he would never break up with his previous one. Robbie mentioned that with that young woman sex had been "more homey," and I could not imagine what that meant. I did not think anything could be much better than the way it was between us in that department — for me the best aspect of our relationship.

Our visit happened to coincide with the royal wedding of Prince Charles and Lady Diana. We spent an exciting day at a pub that displayed the fairytale proceedings on a large screen. Many blocks were cordoned off for dancing in the streets — which we did! But the gray summer days were mostly oppressive and Robbie got the notion to visit some of his old gang who shared a house in Oxford. They pitched a tent for us in the backyard and we melded into the household of three bachelors and one gal who had day jobs and partied and pub-crawled the rest of the time.

The culture of the University town was more to my taste than that of working-class London. The Ashmolean Museum harbors much plunder from ancient civilizations, so I spent time among the reconstructed Egyptian, Assyrian, and Greek temples within its walls. I was reading *The Alexandria Quartet* by British author Laurence Durrell and pondered this quote: "I realized that to become an artist one must shed the whole complex of egotisms which led to the choice of self-expression as the only means of growth! This, because it is impossible, I call The Whole Joke!"

I found a belly dance class and was asked to sub for the teacher when she left on vacation for a couple of weeks. Robbie came along with me the first session but later stayed behind at the house, presumably to have a fling with the pretty female lodger, Sophie. He never admitted to it, but I could literally smell it. I decided not to rock the boat by confronting him and simply let it go by. He had become increasingly moody, sometimes critical and remote and other times high maintenance and needy. The parents of one housemate were excited to have me dance at their garden party, where I brandished my swords among the tables of ladies in floral dresses and frilly summer hats. They were such an enthusiastic audience and paid double the asking price.

As our funds diminished, we sold some of Robbie's stored possessions at the Swiss Cottage flea market in London. Now Robbie arranged to buy a car so we could head for countries with a lower cost of living, namely Portugal. It was a white VW hatchback, steering wheel on the right side. Upon departure, Sophie said, "It will be interesting to see how long you two last," which piqued my possessive instincts and felt like a challenge. We returned to London to say good-bye to Robbie's mum, and then at the end of August 1981 boarded the ferry to Holland.

Leiden and Beyond

"Until you step into the unknown, you don't know what you're made of." Roy T. Bennett

Another of Robbie's friends had settled in The Haag with his wife and children to manage a warehouse of well-polished period carriages and a number of regal horses for the film industry. They put us up in a makeshift guestroom upstairs in the stable. They let us ride the horses, showing me how to "ride English," "post," and "change lead legs," all very different from my previous Western saddle (and bareback) riding experience. Robbie was a complete natural while I struggled to learn.

We stayed with these lovely people for nearly two weeks, exploring a couple of nearby towns. There I first enjoyed *patates frites* with mayonnaise from street kiosks. One day we drove to Amsterdam for my first glimpse of a European hub. I began painting a colorful tropical scene on one side of the white "blank canvas" car, drawing from years of Hawaiian influence.

In an Egyptian restaurant in Leiden, we watched a blond Dutch girl dance. The owner invited me to his home to perform for his family. He proposed that I stay to decorate the interior of the restaurant with Egyptian motifs and become his star dancer. But this was not the Egypt of my goal, so we left, cutting south nonstop through Belgium, then France. I remember breathtaking moonlit views of castles and vineyards along the River Rhone and stopping for a picnic, blackberry picking and lovemaking on a hillside amid tall grass. "When in France…!" We deliberately avoided any major metropolis, car camping our way to Spain, which by contrast seemed stark and dusty.

The Algarve

"The road to success is always under construction."
Lily Tomlin

We picked up a couple of German hitchhikers as we crossed into Northern Portugal, where we stopped at a roadside stand for a bag of oranges. I used my Mexican Spanish, asking for *naranjas* (pronounced nah-*rahng*-hahs). Then the savvy Germans told me that the Portuguese understand Spanish but "don't like it." (Portuguese for oranges is *laranjas* with a soft j).

Resting at a small cafe, I ordered the least expensive item on the menu without suspecting that *dobrades* was a local dish of fava beans laced with tripe, which I could not eat. We soon procured a pocket Berlitz Portuguese-English dictionary I studied diligently.

Again skirting the larger towns, including Lisbon, we passed through cork tree forests, some with the bark peeled away for the main export of Portugal, saw red dragonflies, and pulled into small vineyard roads to rest. We made our way to the Algarve, known for its year around lovely weather and still low cost of living. The word is from the Arabic *al-garb*, meaning the west. The string of coastal fishing villages had been largely built up with hotels and fresh white villas to accommodate the influx of tourists from England,

Germany, and Holland. Many had relocated permanently, and we encountered a large population of English-speaking expats.

Randomly selecting one of these villages far off the main highway, we wound our way down the switchbacks and cliffs to arrive at Praia de Carvoeiro (literally "beach of coal" named for the black pebbles comprising the beach of a small emerald bay). Stopping to get our bearings, we met the Australian owners of a small restaurant and one of the town's notorious Brit expats, Dennis.

We car-camped near the abandoned construction site of an unfinished hotel, using one of the ocean view balconies as a little nest and swimming daily in the gorgeous bay. One day we discovered a "peeping Tom" watching us, so we went straight up to him and said in cobbled-together Portuguese, "In this whole hotel, there is ONE private room!" He slunk away.

Across from the beach was a tasteful arts and crafts gallery run by a Danish woman. Seeing my artwork on both the car and Robbie's shirts, she asked if I could paint a new sign on the window — "Galeria Rosa Maria." As I completed the job, Marietta (her Danish name) suggested I do a painted clothing exhibition to display in the gallery.

We looked for a farmhouse or more permanent accommodations. Our new friend Dennis was caretaker for a friend's villa with a separate guesthouse, which he rented to us for a token amount. I combed the little towns up and down the Algarve for appropriate fabric and set to work, choosing a tropical theme. I employed a local seamstress to help assemble the simple one-size-fits-all resort garments: maxi skirts, easy tunics and kimonos, wrap shorts, scarves, and one "Susie Wong" style long dress of white linen, which I painted with a full-length peacock.

There were other sign jobs as well — a pub called The Legless Arms asked for a sign and tee shirt design, and a realtor needed a special sign for a plot of land up for development. It seemed I was painting full time again. During this period at the mini villa, novice guitar player Robbie plunked away, consistently hitting wrong chords and murdering beloved Beatles songs. Or Dennis would bring a joint and the two of them would joke around while I painted. Robbie more often complained about being ignored or other such phantasms, and we had more spats, which we generally reconciled with our signature deep love-making. But he was getting on my nerves and I began to see him for the loafer he was. Also, Dennis was attractive and always encouraging (though much later revealed himself to be gay).

The day came for the gallery opening — November 5, 1981 — barely one month since our arrival in Praia do Carvoeiro. Due to an article and photo spread which had appeared in the local Algarve Magazine, the place was packed. Among the crowd of partygoers was one serious Lisbon designer who dismissed me, saying "You understand, I am interested only in fashion." I guess this line of home-grown resort wear did not qualify. No matter, I had made trays of hors d'oeuvres and planned to belly dance for the entertainment of the guests. Dennis had agreed to emcee and introduce me. I burst onto the scene with false eyelashes, coins jingling, and finger cymbals ringing, causing quite a stir in the quiet little enclave.

Enough items sold for me to at least recover the cost of materials. But the best outcome of that day for me was when Dennis announced, "I have good news for you dahlin' — you're going belly dancing." Slick schmooze that he was, he knew the owners and managers of all the nightspots throughout the Algarve. As my "agent" he planned to introduce me, and exploit me, to the fullest. For this service, the deal was twenty-five percent of all earnings would go to him, no questions asked, which seemed fair if it resulted in steady dance jobs. He got his boss to loan me his wife's slinky, body-skimming red silk dress for presentation purposes, and soon I had become the sought-after novelty act of the area. Meanwhile the relationship with Robbie had completely deteriorated.

Dennis booked me into a hotel bar for a two-week run, which included a hotel room. By now I was fully ready to break up with Robbie and embark on this dreamed-of career.

He stalked me at the hotel and threatened to kick my teeth in and throw my belongings into the sea. I spent a few nights fearfully cowering in my room, imagining scenes like my body washing up on the shore, trying to meditate. Dennis' boss came to collect his wife's red dress, bring me my bundle of things, and to question me.

Over coffee he said he had believed that Robbie and I really had something and asked if I was sure I wanted to throw it away? When I was adamant, he looked into my eyes and declared "You're just like me; we live on our successes." No comment, as I could not explain the trail of signs and red flags I had ignored during the course of our liaison (writing this now, they seem obvious — from the stolen TV, hiding his U.S. visa status, and the affair in Oxford to the many excuses to avoid working). As my self-proclaimed manager, Dennis himself ended up cajoling Robbie and counseling me to "Be a little flamboyant. The public image is light and happy — save the glum periods for home."

Dennis turned up with a new girlfriend, a Dutch tour guide, saying, "See what I go through for you, dahlin'?" (I had yet to learn he was referring to his preference for men). She certainly was plain-looking but was fluent in Portuguese and had a car. Dennis opportunistically moved into the villa she shared with another lovely Dutch couple, and she willingly helped him comb the Algarve for more dance opportunities for me. By day I stayed mostly in my room practicing finger cymbals and dance exercises.

The next gig was at a restaurant bar which featured week-end live entertainment. The wife had worked in Dutch television and took me aside for a make-over. She taught me how to pluck my eyebrows and use lip liner, admonishing me to "look like an artist at all times." Her subtext was "don't schlep around like an anonymous hippie when not on the job." I have adhered to this advice ever since and never show my face without lip liner!

A retired British RAF pilot, restaurateur, golfer and "social-ite" of the Algarve invited me to occupy the downstairs room of his smaller villa while I danced at a stunning Moorish style hotel in his district. He did not charge rent, did not make physical overtures, and simply appreciated my company. Robbie showed up again, trying to seduce me back. I was ambivalent since there again was that satisfying sex, but the wise sixty-year-old Billie made some pointed comments.

One morning as I did my stretches, he sat nearby reading his newspaper. He exclaimed, "You just did an Olympic workout!" and "Why would you want to be with that deadbeat who is doing nothing? *You* are actually doing *something.*" It is always good to get feedback from friends who can see our blind spots! Around the same time I had philosophical conversations with another male friend. I said I was not sure if I was leading a particularly spiritual life being a belly dancer, to which he replied, "You are the most spiritual person I know."

Dennis was proud to inform me I would be dancing and staying at the prestigious Vilamoura Golf Resort during the Christmas/New Year 1982 season. This place turned out to be where most of the foreign ambassadors to Portugal spent their winter holiday, and it had its own nightclub for the guests. The stage had a Moorish design proscenium, the perfect showcase for a belly dancer. Two quite magical occurrences manifested in that room.

First, the Turkish ambassador and his wife called me over to their table after a performance to inquire where I was from. He had bet his wife that I was from Turkey. That was high praise enough, but then his wife paid me yet another compliment. When I divulged American, she said in French to her husband, "I told you she was too graceful (*trop gracieuse*) to be Turkish."

And second, at the end of the gig the club manager pulled me aside. He gestured over to the bar where Dennis was slumped over a cocktail and asked, "What are you doing with this pimp? Do you realize his drinks are being deducted from your pay? How would you like me to connect you to the best artistic agency in Lisbon?" He soon had me on the phone for a brief interview with an enthusiastic woman who hired me sight unseen on the recommendation of this manager.

Robbie's Gamin Face,
Hawaii 1981

Painted Car from England to Portugal 1981. Dhyanis

Galleria signs, Praia do Carvoeiro, Portugal 1982.
Marietta, Proprietor

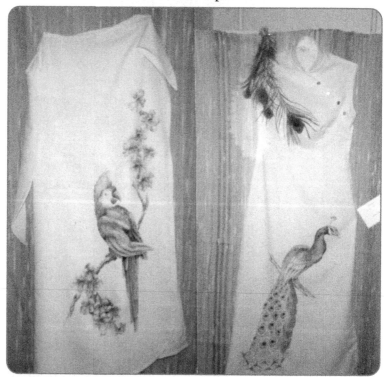

Painted Clothing Exhibition 1982

Interartes

"There is no way to happiness. Happiness is the way."
Wayne Dyer

The agency provided a wide variety of talent to the numerous and very popular nightclubs and *boites* around Portugal and Spain. My first assignment was, conveniently, in Portimao, one of the larger towns in the Algarve.

The owner of the new club was another Danish woman; when I reported to her, she asked if I did *consummation.* Unfamiliar with the term I indignantly said, "No, I am only here to dance." It sounded to me as though it meant to consummate, or have sex with, the customers. She quickly re-phrased to ask if I ever sat to talk and drink with the patrons. When I said yes, she entreated, "Well then, just do what you usually do."

The lodging provided was an apartment to be shared with the other current performers, including a four-person Flamenco troupe from Spain and a stripper, my roommate. Betys was a lovely young woman who had studied ballet and devised some classy strip acts, including one where she began as a sinister witch and gradually transformed into a gorgeous goddess. She spoke no English but willingly tutored me in Portuguese. She had aspirations to become a singer, serenading sweetly from the bath. We were later sent on many gigs together and became fond friends.

The dressing room of that small club doubled as a storage closet for shifting crates of beverages. It was comical with all of us vying for changing space. The flamenco people remained aloof, even slightly hostile, maintaining their superiority. Breakfast at the apartment was usually after noon, as we were all required to stay and "consume" until club closing at three am.

We were being paid directly at the end of each night, which included a few extra escudos as commission on any drinks bought for us by customers. I finally understood the custom of "consummation," though I only accepted drinks and conversation with people I liked, keeping the illusion of freedom and choice as opposed to coercion by the management. One morning around the breakfast table at the apartment the surly Spanish dancer exclaimed, "You can cut anyone else with a knife and nothing happens, but just pinch us and we bleed." I impressed them not at all and could not win them over.

Both Dennis and Robbie came sniffing around, Dennis chatting up Betys, and then the lady club owner. Though Robbie had a way of tugging my heartstrings, my focus was firmly on professionalizing my act and costumes. When Dennis saw me waffling with Robbie he advised, "You have to let go of the past to make room for the future." In continuing correspondence with my British friend Barbara, I mentioned my first impressions of England with Robbie without her (she had remained in Hawaii). Her reply? "I knew he would bugger it up." It turned out to be a drawn-out and dramatic break-up, rife with anguish and so many tears.

The next job from Interartes was scheduled in the northern city of Oporto. A British patron had offered to drive me there in exchange for a seriously artsy photo shoot of me on the roof of his Algarve villa during sunset. I looked so exotic in my costumes — graceful, supple, toned, and tan. The breeze caught my red silk veil and framed my long dark hair and hazel green eyes against the sky.

We arrived in Oporto just in time for me to appear on the tiny circular metallic disco floor of a rather seedy *boite*. The other performer there was a jovial transvestite whose gestures were so exaggeratedly feminine I felt clunky next to him. I stayed in a *pension* recommended by the agency and explored the narrow, cobbled streets and lovely plazas of one of the oldest cities in Europe (on the banks of the Douro River). Delighting in the open markets, I stocked my room with fragrant flowers and fruit.

The second venue in Oporto was the more upper crust Brasilia Club, a classic dinner club with tiered tables, house band, and a curved, red-draped, elevated stage. Prior to the show, I rehearsed on the stage with the curtains open, marking out the space. When it came time to perform, the curtains were closed and I had to find the slit to push through. As the music began, I danced with my usual energetic *mejonce*, or entrance, full speed out through the gap in the curtains to find — there was no stage! The curtains closed not in the center of the curved stage, but at the narrow edge to the side. As I propelled out, I dropped unceremoniously several feet down next to the front table of diners. Embarrassed, I felt two strong men at each side lifting me back up onto the stage where I continued the dance, barely missing a beat with my finger cymbals — my version of "the show must go on"! What a debut. And another lesson learned: find out in advance what the actual stage conditions are to be.

On Sundays all the families of Oporto were out promenading after church; I happily people-watched and window-shopped along with them. There were appealing boutiques displaying fashion-forward ruffled dresses I could not resist. I bought an off-shoulder short black one with a slim gold belt, to which I later hand stitched gold braid trim along each of the ruffles in the style of one of the dance costumes I was creating.

My new routine consisted of waking around noon, walking the town and sewing until applying make-up at 9 pm, then catching a taxi to the venue. Most of these required two shows per night, six nights per week. I felt fantastic. In 1982 I had just celebrated my 35th birthday and was making my living in Europe solely by belly dancing. I found the Portuguese to be "heart people," friendly, helpful, good-natured, family-oriented, and very fond of music and dance.

Lisboa

"Many people will walk in and out of your life, but only true friends will leave footprints in your heart."
Eleanor Roosevelt

At last, Interartes called me for a job in Lisbon where they were based. After taking the train from Oporto, I went directly to their office to meet my benefactors. It was run by an older man and his two partners, both in their late thirties, Artur and Ni, the woman with whom I had originally spoken over the phone from the Algarve. They were truly gracious, well-educated, open-minded people and the chemistry was instant.

Artur was animated by old-world gallantry, fun-loving, and welcoming. He was also level-headed (a great quality when dealing with high-strung artists) and had studied hospitality and hotelery in Switzerland. Pretty Ni bubbled over with playful enthusiasm; she was the ex-wife of the founder and former lover of Artur — liberated woman of Portugal! They welcomed me joyously and were curious about me though they normally did not befriend their artists. They took me into their homes, showed me local sites, added me to their interesting circle of friends, and once they saw me perform, one hundred percent endorsed my dancing.

My Lisbon digs were at a *pension* for artists run by an Indian family from Goa (formerly Portuguese territory). It was on an upper story of an old stone building overlooking a green park surrounding a fountain called Praca da Alegria, or Happiness Square. I wrote long letters, including sketches of this square from my window. Not far away was the big plaza known as Rossio (pronounced Ru-*see*-ou) surrounded by cafes, shops, and a profusion of flower vendors set up around the large twin fountains, which I loved to sketch with a new set of oil pastels.

I was reading the *Diaries of Anais Nin*, a bohemian style woman who had lived on a houseboat along the Seine in Paris among an international set of artists and revolutionaries during the Spanish resistance. One of her lovers was Henry Miller during his broke years writing *Tropic of Cancer* in Paris. I had been catching up on Henry Miller novels since the Algarve. Naturally I too kept a journal, thinking that my adventures might someday merit publishing! After all, one of my favorite quotes from Anais was "We don't see things as they are, we see them as we are," intimating that each of our points of view is unique and valuable.

There was certainly plenty of time for introspection and philosophical ponderings, both alone and with my new friends. I explored the historic town and its many cathedrals and made a point of lighting candles for Serena and my father in every one, feeling this was a way to stay connected to my lost loved ones and past. It was in Lisbon that I first noticed I thoroughly enjoyed my own company and could laugh aloud at my own mental jokes. It also dawned that I truly enjoyed being an independent woman — not attached to any man. I was generally overflowing with vitality, completely open to conversations and self-discovery. My agent, Artur, orchestrated the correct legal paperwork so that I was registered as a working artist, even paying taxes through the agency, so I was legally secure in Portugal.

Having purchased a small cassette tape player, I could reset my music for each night's show (sometimes starting mid-tape) to hand to the DJ. I continued to change up my repertoire of costumes and props. In general this was unorthodox among the performers who usually repeated the same act every night for the entire run of anywhere from one week to two months. I also enjoyed listening to cassettes of the World Class Brazilian singer Maria Bettania and learned the lyrics of her sensual songs. My favorite album was "*Mel*" (Honey) and my favorite song was "*Abelha Rainha*" (Queen Bee); and I practically wore out those tapes singing along. The teenage Indian daughter at the *pension* sat with me to help translate and practice her English.

Out of town I often worked and roomed with Betys. We were sent to the island of Madeira south of Portugal and approximately 450 miles off the coast of Morocco. The prominent nightspot in the port town of Funchal, The Safari Club, was run by a powerful French woman. She allowed us to drink passion fruit drinks without alcohol, though the customers were not supposed to know it when they paid for our "cocktails" and the privilege of our company. Many tourists stopped in there and I particularly liked a sensitive British fellow, traveling with his divorced father. They took me around the island in their rental car and on steep hikes around the cliffs and down into the central terraced farm-lands of once-volcanic Madeira. Although Madeira's history includes export of both wheat and sugar, it now looks like any tropical paradise. The streets are lined with purple blooming jacaranda trees and the main export is the syrupy Madeira wine.

On the Atlantic coast of Portugal, 35 kilometers west of Lisbon at Guincho stands a stone fort which hosts Renaissance-themed dinners. Artur and Ni booked me to dance at these exclusive soirees along with a magician and his wife. They worked hard to keep me employed, know-ing that I did not like to rest between club gigs. The plum nightclub of the city, Maxime's, was situated a block off the other side of "my" Praça da Alegria, bordering the theater section. I was thrilled when Interartes booked me there. As a cabaret it had been a hot spot for spies and resistance during the 1940s war years and looked the part. It had a dark, heavy wood bar and furniture, red plush booths, mirrored pillars, and a white marble stage with a shimmering silver curtain.

Now Maxime's seemed to be the Portuguese Mafia meeting place. There was a house band and the artists were required to dance with the clients between sets. Many of the customers were expert at ballroom partnering, so I quite enjoyed it. There were also "B Girls" whose job was to keep the patrons drinking. They were adept at surreptitiously emptying their glass under the table. The few times I tried this I got caught, so I actually had to drink liberal amounts of whiskey poured from the bottles on each table. Later Interartes got me work as an extra in films, including one Terry Garr movie, about the war intrigue in Portugal — *To Catch a King*. The scene I was in was filmed inside Maxime's and I was costumed, with professional hair and make-up, as a glamorous forties woman conversing with a young uniformed soldier in one of the red booths. I felt like I had a secret, having formerly danced on that marble stage!

Ni gave me a key to her apartment outside of Lisbon where I sometimes had dinner ready for her, Artur, and a few friends when they returned from their work day. They especially liked my ratatouille, vegetables simmered in a garlicky tomato wine sauce, layered with melted cheese. Once Artur was incredulous when he noticed I had used some of their more expensive wine in the dish. I laughingly argued that one needs good ingredients to end up with a good meal, and all was forgiven. These people felt like family. Also during time off from dancing I painted a mural of purple wisteria vines on Ni's white bedroom wall, and hand-painted decorative pillows for the apartment.

At Maxime's I had made friends with another dancer/
stripper who offered me her family's extra apartment a twen-
ty-minute train ride west of Lisbon and a steep windy walk
to the top of a hill. The rules were "no men, and do not enter
the master bedroom." I accepted the deal, moved there, and
managed to break the pact on only three occasions! During
this time I also put up notices at the nearby train station
offering English tutoring services. A family who was being
transferred to the U.S. hired me to work with their ten-year-
old son to help prepare him for American schools.

At one point I contracted a high fever and could not get
out of bed for several days. There was no phone in the
apartment, so I crawled to the elevator, down one floor to a
neighbor I knew to be a doctor. He and his wife took pity on
me and got me some medicine. The doctor diagnosed me
with rheumatic fever and said I should not be climbing that
hill from the train station, exposed to wind and rain, or I
would relapse. In thanks I painted a sign for the wife's florist
shop window, and as far as I know, never had a recurrence of
that ailment.

Interartes found me a job in a discotheque style nightclub
in Spain, and though I was quite comfortable traveling by
train around Portugal, Artur decided to drive me there. On
the way we passed fields of purple garlic flowers (I had to
pick some) and he took me to lunch at a castle converted
to a five-star hotel and restaurant. The white-gloved waiters
hovered around anticipating every need and making us feel
like royalty.

As we talked, I was suddenly and unexpectedly seduced by
Artur, normally quite an unassuming figure. After my performance that night, it felt right to share a bed and become
more intimate friends. He was very tender and divulged that
he had been hoping for this since our first meeting. He made
it clear that he expected nothing; we were both quite free to
follow other passions but profoundly enjoyed each other's
company.

Snake Dance, Fire Dance

"I like pushing boundaries." Lady Gaga

In Lisbon I danced at one Cafe Concerto for the young and hip. It stood across the narrow, cobbled street from an antique shop where the owner kept a large boa constrictor in a glass cage displayed in the front window. When the owner, Andre, saw me dance, he offered the snake for my act. I was also teaching a summer intensive belly dance class in the same neighborhood, *Bairo Alto,* so I visited him and handled the snake to test our "chemistry."

Experimenting with the snake, I found that if I danced under a large potted palm, its head and body would rise up into the air. I could do a backbend with the snake looped around my waist under the tree, and the snake would muscle its way upright through the air, creating quite an effect. However one night a girl in the crowd burst into hysterical screams, so I danced the snake out the door and back to its cage across the street.

Andre was an artistic gay man with connections to a rhinestone costume maker, so we designed a chunky rhinestone bra and belt set for me in the style of 1920s Art Deco, or Mata Hari. It was from him that I first learned about the rampant AIDS epidemic; he said he was worried about his habit of beachcombing for partners. There he discovered a gorgeous twenty-something, ebony-skinned soccer player from Cape Verde who was willing to join my act at the cafe. I choreographed a *pas-de-deux* and costumed him like a pharaoh's guard. For a few shows he effortlessly lifted me into the air and posed while I danced (and Andre hit on him).

Interartes hired two of my students along with me and the snake for a feria (street fair) near the beach. We audaciously draped the six-foot creature over the three of us, wrapping and unwrapping him around ourselves in a sinuous choreography. This was a memorable *spectaculo* we repeated for the Cafe Concerto crowd, and my students were thrilled to actually get paid for dancing.

In a Lisbon curio shop I "scored" an intact piece of silver-hammered black mesh fabric from Egypt (called Assiut, after the town which produces it). This became a tunic to wear over silvery harem pants for a new fire dance. I also found three Chinese hardwood plate-holders, inserted them with tin cups to hold a cotton wick. Lamp oil provided fuel for the steady flames. I balanced one on my head while manipulating the other two with expansive "snake arm" movements. Only once during floorwork did a breeze from offstage cause the flame to dip down and singe my hair. The audience gasped, there was a pungent odor, and I had a new hairstyle with shorter bangs.

Morocco – First Flavor of Araby

"The soul of the Universe is nourished by people's happiness." Paulo Coelho

My mother faithfully forwarded *Habibi Belly Dance Magazine* to me, care of Lisbon General Delivery. In it was an ad for a dancer's tour in Morocco, south of Portugal 500 miles across the Atlantic. Portugal is closer to Morocco than to Egypt, my ultimate destination. Knowing that this dance is also part of Moroccan culture, it made sense to take advantage of the proximity and further my dance education. I booked a flight to the meeting point in Casa Blanca a few days earlier than the tour was to begin. The small plane was so rickety you could see loose bolts bouncing on the wings during the bumpy one-and-a-half-hour trip.

I took my camera into the streets, positively vibrating with the excitement of touching ground in my first Arabic country. I casually snapped a photo of two women in black burqas resting on a street corner with a donkey cart. Immediately, out of nowhere, a pack of boys appeared, yelling and pelting pebbles at me. I ran for my life until I encountered some gendarmes who turned the aggressive boys back! Here was my first lesson about the fundamentalist Islamic culture, how women are vigorously protected from public view.

The dance tour was led by a New York personality — dancer, scholar and educator — who called herself "Morocco" or "Aunt Rocky." She ensured our safety by requiring us to cover up from head to toe with long dresses, long sleeves and headscarves. Anything less, she told us, would be disrespectful, not to mention advertise us as Western trollops. She brought us to restaurants where the dancers who performed would pull us onto the floor and encourage us to imitate their specialties — some of our most authentic lessons!

We took a train south to Marrakech through the reddish countryside dotted with huge sculptural clay water towers. It was June, when Marrakech hosted an annual Music and Dance Festival at the palace grounds. The ceremony opened with Berber horsemen galloping in, twirling rifles overhead, and dancing their impeccable steeds in formation to the cracking drum beats. Then, one at a time, groups of women from all around the country emerged from the surrounding tents, dressed in their local folk costumes, to demonstrate their local village variation of "the dance." Many linked arms or held each other's waists undulating together, simul-taneously executing intricate footwork. The bright color combinations were stunning. One group from the Berber Atlas wore long green dresses layered with multiple neck-laces of chunky amber, brilliant orange hip sashes, and sparkling metallic headdresses. I tried to notate the many rhythms and steps, but the variety was mind-boggling.

Aunt Rocky took us to see the *Schikatt,* traditional wedding dancers considered educated women who recited poetry as well as initiated young brides into the sexual arts. They were fully covered but exuded playfulness and sensuality with their movements. In the Marrakech *souk,* or market-place, she warned us to stay together, holding hands so as not to get lost or abducted from the group. I could not help but make eye contact with a rugged, passing Berber in his long brown and cream striped *galabeya* (hooded, robe-like garment). Whip fast, his hand shot out to grab my breast. I let out a startled screech and the other girls pulled me along through the crowd. My Western boldness had elicited immediate feedback, but I could hardly help but look into those steely grey sexy desert eyes.

In that same souk, Rocky led us to her favorite cloth vendor where we all purchased bright new veil and skirt fabric. Mahmoud the proprietor invited us all to his home to join in his celebration of his baby son's christening. We felt privileged to enter through the gate of one of the high, windowless walls lining the streets to the Arabian Nights paradise within. Growing inside the large tiled courtyard were orange trees and other flowering shrubs. The house itself was a U-shaped two-story building with carved wooden screens open to the courtyard. We ate in one of the upstairs rooms behind the screen on low cushioned benches around a large low table. We were shown how to make cous-cous balls with our fingers to scoop up the lamb *tagine* and other savory dishes directly from the serving platters. The young ladies of the family were proud to speak some English and tell us they were attending university. At that time (1983) Morocco had a progressive faction which acknowledged the importance of the education of women.

Out in the main square amid cobra charmers, stork nests perched high on the "minarets and parapets," and open sacks of pungent spices, I bought a colorful, tall conical bread basket. We took a small plane to Tangiers and to save space I wore the cone on my head. Aunt Rocky turned around in her seat and said in her broad New York accent, "She even looks good in a bread basket!"

In Tangiers we enjoyed the celebrated French-Arabic cuisine and the more European atmosphere layered onto the city by the former French colonialists. There were also older maze-like sections of winding, narrow earthen streets known as the *casbah*. These were sprinkled with specialty vendors of treasures such as amber amulets or sets of the decorated glasses used to serve sweetened mint tea, served everywhere. One could just make out the Straits of Gibraltar which led from the Atlantic into the Mediterranean Sea. It was easy to imagine the ancient Moors sailing across the nine-mile stretch of water to invade Spain and Portugal, leaving their mark on the language and architecture of both countries.

Double Sword Dance in Portugal, 1982

Portugal Friends 1982. Agents Ni second from left,
Artur bottom right

Lisbon, Rio Tejo (River Tagus) 1983. Ni and D

Snake Dance (Photo from 1989)

Fire Dance, with Assiut Tunic, Portugal 1983

Funchal, Madeira 1983. Betys and Dhyanis with locals

Tangiers, Morocco 1983. Dhyanis with Gnawi Dancers

Encore Tour

*"I love to walk a city, whether I've been there once or a
hundred times before. It's amazing what sort of inspiration
you'll find when you steal a second glance."*
Erin Hienstra

I returned to Lisbon with fresh dance energy and a bag full
of the small silver-toned disks punched with a hole in the
center of each, typically found dangling from Moroccan
head and hip scarf tassels. For Artur's birthday in August,
I embroidered a white silk scarf with his favorite flower, a
fuchsia, and added a spangled Moroccan style fringe. I also
presented him with other gifts representing his favorite pastimes (a pack of tennis balls, a bottle of good wine). When
he saw all this he wept, saying, "You spent your last escudo
on me, not knowing when you would earn more."

He was right, I needed more work. Interartes started send-
ing me on their circuit for the second time around. I worked
again in Oporto, the Algarve, and Maxime's in Lisbon.
There some of the patrons believed I was only pretending
to be American since my Portuguese had become quite
fluent. An American man made a date for lunch to ask me if
I was interested in becoming a spy. He accused me of being
"unpatriotic" when I refused that dangerous-sounding offer.
I doubt anyone could fathom I was traveling alone and

spending time performing in nightclubs solely for the love of the dance.

Back for the second time at the Safari Club on Madeira, I met Sandy Mars, a girl from New York with a roller-skating strip act. She created her own soft-sculpture costumes (gloved hands on her bra which she could manipulate with strings to open and close in peek-a-boo fashion, jungle foliage with large movable leaves, etc.). We spent afternoons together hand-stitching and talking. She had been working in Greece and thought I would be perfect for one of the nightclubs in Athens. She promised to recommend me to the owner, saying "Oh, Yanni will *love* you!" For me this represented advancing another step along the path of "dancing my way to Egypt" and fresh new adventure.

Meanwhile that month in Funchal I played out a drama with the young heir to a hillside vineyard estate. He was an amateur singer and took me to after-hours bars where he got the orchestra to play while he sang to me the romantic Billy Joel song "I Love You Just the Way You Are." He shared bottles of Madeira dated 1896 from his deceased parents' cellar as I acted hostess, staging elegant dinners for his friends at his family home. It was quite the fantasy as he was long-betrothed to a college girl from a neighboring family who was at the time away studying in Lisbon. The girl caught wind of our affair and he left to assuage her, telling me, "The girl is going crazy." I found all this out after we had formed our liaison but thoroughly enjoyed this second time on the island with a native, rather than as a tourist.

Greece

"We are what we repeatedly do. Excellence, then, is not an act, but a habit." Aristotle, 4th century BC

When, in the fall of 1983, the message came from Sandy saying that Yanni would hire me on her recommendation, I left a box of accumulated Portuguese memorabilia with Ni and Artur, packed up my costumes, and was met at the airport by Yanni himself. He vouched for my temporary artist's visa, and drove me straight to his club, *Le Chat Noir*. He was a fiftyish ex-merchant marine, very rough around the edges. Right away he told me that Sandy no longer worked for him because she did not participate in "consummation." My heart sank a bit if this is what I had to look forward to. He ordered me upstairs to the dressing room to change and go onstage immediately. I opened the show that night as the lowest in the hierarchy of performers, more or less like an audition. The second night I found myself last in the line-up, the star spot.

A friend of Yanni's, John, a former singer at the club, saved me from Yanni's clutches. He was a handsome half-Greek, half-British sophisticated gay man who was turning his nearby apartment into an artist's dorm. That first week in Athens I helped him shop for discount fabric and sew the curtains and sheets to outfit the room with three single beds lined up in a row. I also decorated the walls with beautiful Art Deco prints of "The Seasons" by Alphonse Mucha. Soon I had an international parade of dancer roommates.

Working in Greece was far more competitive than in Portugal. Here East meets West and there is a much larger population of itinerant Middle Eastern businessmen at the clubs, as well as more dancers from Middle Eastern countries. There was also much more emphasis on selling alcohol and I was instructed to cajole the clients into ordering bottles of champagne between shows if they wanted to sit and talk with me. The popular blond "B Girls" hailed from countries like Germany and Sweden. Earning money to send back to their families, they did not want to share "their" clients with me. One fellow reported to me that those girls were claiming I was "old — and a lesbian." However one of the girls, Violet, had a somewhat innocent younger customer becoming infatuated with her (which did not fit her plan to snag a rich sugar daddy), and she sent him over to me. Charming and funny, twenty-nine-year-old Costas was from the more provincial Peloponnese and now worked as a palace guard in the center of Athens. We became genuinely friendly and double-dated with Sandy Mars and her more intellectual Greek boyfriend. Costas' quirky mind always made me laugh. Later, when I decided to move into his apartment, John assessed him as "rather immature."

I was blind to this, but a later incident at the Athens Museum proved it a correct assessment. Costas proudly boasted he had learned in school that Greece was the oldest civilization, full stop. He was dismayed to compare the dates of the antiquities. When he saw that Egypt and several other entire civilizations pre-dated that of the Greeks, he stormed out of the museum in a huff, walking on the opposite side of the street.

Another time we took a ferry from Piraeus to visit some of the smaller islands on the beautiful green Aegean Sea not far from Athens, and we really had a great time hiking the steep pathways of the small towns. It was near Easter and we watched the spectacular Greek Orthodox custom of candle-light processions winding their way up to the church. And as usual I lit my own candles for my daughter and father, always remembering that it was Good Friday the day they died.

My New York friend Sandy revealed that she "did tricks" with old men willing to pay $500 for twenty minutes with her. She was amassing money in a Swiss bank account and planning to buy a loft with living space and an art studio when she returned to New York. She tried to convince me it was easy and to join her. Aside from outright disgust at the idea, I was seriously working on a career in dance and wanted nothing to damage it. I was adamant about elevating the art of belly dance out of the realm of "hootchie-kootch" or stripping, much less prostitution. I reasoned that if someone were to recognize me, both my reputation would be ruined and the dance would be sullied. John told me, "Sandy is not worried about her career, only her fanny," a British term referring to the female genitalia; but amassing money was her true goal.

One older Greek gentleman, a doctor, asked me to join a group "for breakfast," since in summertime the clubs closed at 4 am and people were hungry. He took me aside and asked, "What's your price?" When I smilingly told him I was not in the game, he insisted "Come on — *everyone* has their price" and tried to tempt me after the meal with expensive clothing in the boutique windows near the restaurant. I think he was truly perplexed by my definitive stand.

Another Greek belly dancer invited me to her apartment for lunch of delicious lemon chicken soup and to watch videos of famous Egyptian dancers. I absorbed everything on those videos, especially Nagua Fouad borne onto the stage in a palanquin, stepping out to dance in an all-gold costume covered with moving paillettes. Also captivating was Azza Sharif in a fully covered green folkloric costume with red and gold accents, with such bold hip movements followed around by her musicians as she danced her way around a fountain. Aspiring belly dancers the world over devoured these iconic images! But I felt that my hostess invited me only to brag that she had an American friend. In general I found the Greek people not as friendly and truly accepting of foreigners but extremely nationalistic. I had been spoiled by my exceptional friends in Portugal.

A well-known American dancer, Rhea of California, had been living and working in Athens for many years. There she raised her two daughters (also beautiful dancers) and together they monopolized the tourist area of the *Plaka,* moving between the three or four restaurants and *bouzoukia* nightly. I knocked at her door, though we had never met. She greeted me with the ambivalent declaration, "Come in — God must have sent you to me for *some* reason." Our relationship evolved and we witnessed each other's shows. She brought me to perform at a luncheon for the American Women's Club, announcing that our styles were completely opposite; mine was like a cool drink of water while hers was fiery like a gypsy. I took a few private classes to incorporate some of her fire, learning new Greek techniques, which I still teach and perform these 35 years later. She lived near the Acropolis so I was invited to use her brightly painted apartment as a dressing room for a photo shoot on the hill in front of the Parthenon.

For my next gig at the famed Olympia Club, I needed professional photos for the marquee on the street. The result was a series of photos in different costumes which captured me at my peak, and I sent copies back to Interartes in Lisbon. At the more prestigious Olympia Club, I befriended a new cast of entertainers including a Moroccan native belly dancer, a sympathetic Romanian "Ballet" troupe, and the "peaches and cream" English Contemporary Dancer, Vanessa. She had a Palestinian boyfriend and a horrific tale of them being arrested and jailed as spies in Lebanon (for wearing matching star of David pendants). We shared lunches, our main meal of the day, at the neighborhood *tavernas.* Her act was an emotional, high-kicking modern dance, in a wispy blue chiffon tunic and thong, set to the Phil Collins song "In the Air Tonight." Her agent had contacts throughout the Middle East and encouraged her to learn everything she could from me; he planned to send her out with a new talent as a belly dancer herself. She was sent to Syria where she studied with a male teacher to perfect the art. Years later she brought her husband and new baby to visit me in Northern California. She danced a set at the Egyptian restaurant where I worked, the Cairo Cafe, and I thought she was perfect.

I often spent time at the closest beach in Piraeus, the port town adjoining Athens, where ferries crossed back and forth to all the islands. It was there I first tasted the delicacy of grilled octopus. I brought my beadwork and stretched out on the sand to keep up my golden tan. There I met a tourist belly dancer from Georgia, Farrashah. We both were scheduled to audition at a Syrian restaurant with a live band. As we took our turns, I prayed to land the job, figuring I needed it more than this dancer on vacation. They did choose me and had me dance at a wedding reception in the restaurant the next week. The guests lifted me onto a long table and kept me shimmying there with my sword balanced on my head for several songs. As is customary in both Greece and the Middle East, tipping is done by scattering paper bills over the dancer's head, and that night I was showered with money.

John, the Brit/Greek singer, introduced me to a dancing duo who resembled Aphrodite and Adonis. Kristina and Yanni were forming a small dance company to tour in the north and asked me to join. We rehearsed in their spacious Athens apartment where they taught me a part in a modern jazz trio with them, gave me the role of samba dancer to accompany a Brazilian song sung by John, plus had me perform my double sword specialty solo. The show finale was a spectacular *pas de deux* by the idyllic couple.

We were booked for a month at a large, festive *bouzoukia* in Xanthi at the extreme northeastern tip of Greece bordered by Bulgaria and Turkey. The outdoor market in the main square was teeming with women wearing *salwar,* or full-legged cotton pantaloons gathered at the ankle, a more practical version of what we term harem pants, and the ubiquitous headscarves. The delicious varieties of olives and fresh bread made the perfect lunch. I was infatuated with a young Greek singer and learned his signature song (he had a ferociously jealous Greek girlfriend so I never got too close); and as I had in Portugal, gathered most of my best language skills from popular songs.

One afternoon I was hired for a solo gig at a special outdoor event. The partygoers plied me with celebratory shots of ouzo with predictably disastrous consequences. At the show that evening I was completely off balance and my swords kept slipping. Kristina and Yanni were appalled, saying I should have bowed out of the show if I could not handle it. The uncontrollable vertigo had surprised me too but served as another reminder to stay sober.

We crossed the border to visit a Turkish market town, which looked hardly different from the Greek town of Xanthi. It was like stepping back in time to witness donkey carts, turbans, and dust everywhere.

Crete

"The last western society to worship female powers was Minoan Crete. And significantly, that fell and did not rise again." Camille Paglia

Not having an official agent in Greece, I got jobs only by referral. I was invited to a hotel in Heraklion (Iraklio) on the island of Crete to dance improvisationally with their Greek Bouzouki (Greek lute) Band. I stayed two weeks, then was moved to a club at the other end of the island near Chania (pronounced Ha-*nyah*). At the fourteenth century Venetian port there is a World War II monument to the bravery of the Greek farmers who had awaited the parachuting Germans and defended the island with nothing more than pitchforks.

Of special interest to me was the Palace of Knossos where the legendary King Minos had kept his half bull, half man son, The Minotaur in the underground Labyrinth. It was said anyone who entered there would be forever lost and killed by the Minotaur. The king's daughter, Ariadne, for love of the mythical hero Theseus, provided him with a silver thread to find his way in and out of the Labyrinth to slay the Minotaur. In typical Greek tragedian form, Theseus then abandoned Ariadne.

The Minoan civilization was at one time powerful with centuries of layers built one on top of the other. There women had been respected for their roles in the discovery of agriculture and invention of the arts of weaving and pottery making. It was also the origin of the iconic dancing Snake Priestess image we know, holding up a writhing snake in each hand, symbol of protection of the house in the ancient Minoan religion.

The Chania nightclub was a bit rough. Another dancer stole my prized Egyptian Assiut tunic from the dressing room and I found myself out of a job. I could only assume that she had seniority at the club and perhaps was jealous. I was of course disappointed but still so grateful to spend a whole month exploring the island.

Egypt – Motherland of the Dance

"The disciple must experience in himself each stage of developing. And he will know nothing for which he is not ripe." Karnak Temple

By now, approaching my thirty-seventh birthday early in 1984 and after some four years of dancing abroad, I had saved enough drachma to attain my goal of traveling to Egypt. This proved good timing, as I saw a new ad for an upcoming dance tour led again by the knowledgeable Aunt Rocky, this time to Egypt. I had met a couple of Syrian students who traded on the black market and sold me U.S. dollars for the trip.

This time I booked the flight allowing an extra week after the tour was to end. I arrived at the old Victoria Hotel in Cairo at midnight where Rocky was waiting up to give me her "orientation" speech. I pulled my wad of cash out of my boot and paid her, and she showed me upstairs to my designated room. She had randomly paired off those of us traveling singly. Dorothea of Boston and I immediately bonded as if sisters. She was breaking free from an oppressive marriage and to her I represented courageous freedom — "like a butterfly" she later wrote about me in her poetry.

Rocky again had us dress conservatively in long dresses (I now had my embroidered *galabeya*, the long robe-like garment purchased in Tangiers) with covered heads and sturdy footwear. Most of us dangerous dancers managed to exude an irrepressible sensuality in spite of these precautions! Some were uninhibitedly provocative when we had opportunities to dance together on open stages. For our itinerary, Rocky had bought blocks of tickets for us to see the large dance productions popular in the eighties. We were in awe of all the big stars of the videos we had hungrily devoured. Nagua Fouad, Souher Zaki, Fifi Abdo and Nadia Hamdi were at the top of the list with their back-up dancers, many costume changes, and singing and joking with the audience.

We had classes with the famous choreographer Mahmoud Reda, who had adapted and elevated many of the regional folk styles for the stage. He required his young performers to study ballet to add posture and grace to the earthy dances. His dance company became the gold standard of Egyptian dance, which he toured around the world. His Reda Dance Company had appeared at Carnegie Hall, Covent Garden, and other prestigious opera houses. From him I learned my first "Saidi" (region of Upper Egypt) cane dance, a version of which I taught at a workshop at Columbia College (California) on a visit to the U.S. later on.

We boarded a train that followed the Nile River upstream, south to Luxor (ancient Thebes) in "Upper Egypt." Upon arrival, Dorothea and I hailed a horse-drawn carriage to the rambling ruins of Karnak, the ancient center of worship of Amun-Ra the sun god, to watch the sunset.

A jovial man in a white turban and long black *galabeya* jumped up onto the front buckboard with the driver, turned to us and said, "I'm your entertainment for tonight." We made friends with this fellow, Osman, one of the musicians Rocky had hired for us that evening, also expert at dancing with a beer bottle balanced upright on his head. The next night I conspired with Dorothea to cover for me if Rocky found me missing from our room, so I could meet with Osman. He hoped I could recommend his band to work in Athens. He also mentioned he was accompanying us back to Cairo and knew of a place I could stay after the group departed.

In Luxor we danced with the Banat Mazim, daughters of the only remaining Ghawazi family, who preserved the lineage of a special branch of folk dance. We also ventured into the desert to explore subterranean tombs in the Valley of the Kings with their still-vivid wall paintings. We saw the Colossus of Memnon and walked inside the palace of Hatchepsut, Pharaoh Queen, with whom we all identified. Dorothea and I took a ride on a *feluka*, or small Egyptian square-sailed boat, up the Nile to Banana Island. As we walked among the fruit plantations, we passed a crippled beggar seated along the path. I turned to witness Dorothea holding her palms out in a gesture of blessing — and saw blue light miraculously radiating from her hands. I was discovering the deeper qualities of my new friend. Her empathy makes her a natural healer, and she later studied to become a Reiki Master and hypnotherapy practitioner.

We were truly on a magical pilgrimage together, the culmination of a longtime dream for both of us. Dorothea had no funds for the trip but claimed that her deceased mother sent signs (consisting of roses) encouraging her to commit anyway. The money had manifested in surprising ways and now we saw more 'signs of the rose' everywhere. There was a fragrant rose garden outside our Luxor hotel room, and once back in Cairo inside a chamber of the Great Pyramid, Dorothea found a dried rose in an otherwise empty stone sarcophagus.

At Giza we took the obligatory camel riding photos and saw the impressive light show and dance ensemble at the tourist center there. Rocky took us to the old neighborhood Khan El Khalili, Cairo's equivalent of the Grand Bazaar, guiding us to Mahmoud's Haberdashery stocked with beaded scarves and dance costumes. On my slim budget I bought a used dress that Rocky had for sale — red with all-over gold beaded fringe. When we hugged good-bye, little did Dorothea and I suspect we would return to Egypt together to dance at the 1990 wedding of my Egyptian boss at the Cairo Cafe in California.

Now though, contrary to all of Aunt Rocky's admonitions, I was in Cairo alone with an Egyptian man — a musician no less. He took me to a barely furnished apartment with crumbling plaster walls where several of his musician friends joined us. I spent most of my remaining Egyptian pounds on modest meals for this group and they took me to see a film with a short dance scene they thought I would like (though my understanding of Arabic was too meager to appreciate the plot). Each night the guys produced instruments and gathered to play on the steps of the apartment building.

I had nothing to do but dance. At first I was shy about it but gradually the music cast its spell and I let it flow through me in a whole new way, discovering a freedom of movement there on the marble entryway. Here was the breakthrough I had hoped for, since first conceiving this wild idea of "dancing my way to Egypt." All the study and skills acquired along the way were valuable, but this was an exhilarating new level of feeling in the moment, one with the people's music. This was a revelation — experimenting with the movement — somehow becoming more myself and happening right here in a nondescript neighborhood in the Motherland of the Dance!

Osman and his crew accompanied me to the Greek Embassy where I needed to apply for a visa to get back into Greece. Walking along the crowded chaotic streets of Cairo, I felt the weight of my shoulder bag lighten and caught a pickpocket in the act. I slapped his hand away indignantly and looked to Osman for protection. He simply shrugged, unperturbed, as if this were to be expected.

It was good to have help navigating the Arabic bureaucracy and I was finally seated at a desk with a telephone. I called the number of the Olympia Club in Athens to ask if they would guarantee me a job upon return. Amazingly the manager agreed and I was issued the correct work visa to return to Greece. I also tried to pitch the Egyptian band to entertain at the club, but the manager was not ready for that.

The plumbing was iffy at the dilapidated apartment and proper hygiene was difficult. I ended up paying for the "free rent" with a painful bladder infection which I endured silently for days before the flight out. I had told Osman I would give him whatever Egyptian money I had left. At the airport he was incredulous when I produced only about 14 paltry Egyptian pounds. I'm sure he and his buddies assumed I was a rich American and they would be well-compensated for taking care of me that week. I was sorry I could not give more but was truly returning to Greece penniless.

The cultural and spiritual enrichment I had received was, however, beyond measure. There is an important untranslatable Arabic word, *tarab,* popular among musicians and dancers. The closest concept might be ecstasy from the Greek, meaning "to go outside of oneself" into some intense euphoric experience or "zone." It was certain that I had experienced *tarab* in the Motherland of the Dance.

Savoring the Cherries: Island of Crete 1984

Parthenon, Athens, Greece 1984

Giza, Egypt 1984. Dreams Come True

Luxor, Egypt 1984. Felucca on the Nile

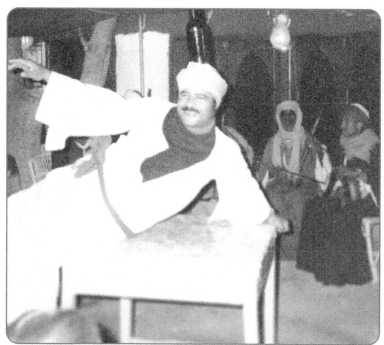

Luxor, Egypt 1984. Osman's beer bottle balancing dance

Cairo, Egypt 1984.
Dorothea enjoying Rebaba music at the souq

New Trajectory

*"Nobody can go back and start a new beginning, but any-
one can start today and make a new ending."*
Maria Robinson

Greek boyfriend Costas met me at the airport and took me
to a clinic for medication which worked instantly. He had
been sweet and polite with me and did not ask much about
Egypt. When my American dancer friend Rhea offered to
introduce me to a new Arabic club in town, he came along.

I danced open floor to the band playing a well-known 9/8
rhythm song, a specialty derived from Turkish Romany
gypsy music, quite differently accented from the evenly
divided phrases of the more commonly played eight-count
phrases. The manager seemed interested but wanted me to
formally audition.

As I prepared my costume at the appointed time, Costas
barred the door to his apartment and reverted to caveman.
He believed the audition was an excuse, and the manager
only wanted an "assignation" with me. He even threatened
to burn all my costumes. In order to calm him down I
submitted and treated him gently, rather than fighting. But I
soon moved out of his apartment and into the artists' dorm
where Vanessa lived. Her manager got me a job in a club
with her.

I received two bits of diverse news. Artur of Interartes Agency in Lisbon called to say that on the strength of the new photos, he had gotten me a contract to dance in a hotel in Dubai. He knew how much dancing in an Arabic country would please me. It was not until October, still months away, but I was elated.

Also, my mother had forwarded an invitation to my twenty-year high school reunion in California coming up in August. I called the organizer to propose that I would fly all the way from Greece only if I could dance at the reunion party. He said it could be arranged, so after all these years, I was to return "home" for a two-week visit with a round-trip ticket back to Athens, of course, to await the Dubai date.

High School Reunion

"We must be willing to let go of the life we have planned so as to accept the life that is waiting for us." Joseph Campbell

I stayed with Mom and was pleased to see that she had a new man in her life, of Greek heritage. He was an ex-naval officer with a career in landscape architecture, and with whom Mom shared her love of gardening and co-owned a sailboat and a small plane. She was a great role model, learning to fly at 61 years of age!

My oldest friend from grammar school through high school picked me up for the reunion and we enthusiastically circulated among our classmates. Most had not changed over the twenty years. I felt I had become a whole different person from the bookish "good student" most had known me to be. I had thought in those days that to be part of the popular crowd, one spoke in clever repartee as scripted in the movies. So I had remained silently humiliated, composing those scripts in my head but always too late. It was difficult to figure out how to relate in school as I did naturally within my family. I had sewn my own version of the latest fashions, hiked up my skirts, and done all the things of which my mother disapproved but still gained no social acceptance outside my small circle of less cool friends (who are now joyously back in my life).

After I danced the sword-balancing number on the reunion stage, it seemed few recognized me. But I did connect with some. One man, Dick, I had "liked" for years or, in fact had obsessed over in endless private fantasies, had married his high school sweetheart and become a U.S. military officer. I felt safe enough now to confess my longtime crush. He replied, "Really? But you seemed so hostile." Recalling a time I saw him while shopping with our mothers at the grocery store, my mom had entreated, "Why not say hi?" Instead, I hid behind the vegetables. Maybe paralyzed shyness could be construed as hostility.

Another fellow who had "liked" *me* in senior year commercial art class made overtures. In high school I had considered him not up to my standards due to acne and thick glasses, but Robert had improved with age. He had actually spent some time in the Arabic Gulf States on business. He asked me out and we spent time together, at the end of which he asked, "What will it take to get you back here, Carniglia?" The plan we conceived was that I would return to Greece and work until the Dubai contract was done. After that I would meet him in Italy. He had studied architecture in Florence, spoke fluent Italian, our common heritage, and had family to visit there. I had yet to experience Italy and he said he would happily show me around.

I flew back to Greece to await the anticipated Dubai gig. Robert had connected me with some Dutch friends of his now living in Greece. They took me windsurfing on a lake and we talked about Robert. The wife told me how he cooked pasta with obsessive care, stirring the pot "like a baby." I wondered if by comparison I was not meticulous enough. A lot seemed to ride on this relationship as it meant a complete change of lifestyle for me, and we did not really know that much about each other's habits. At least I knew we came from similar backgrounds.

But the jobs were more scarce. I found only weekend nights at a *bouzoukia* in Piraeus. One night when I arrived the owner had me sit at her table and asked, "Do you have a red dress?" Indeed I had left the beaded Egyptian gown on a hook in the dressing room. She pointed to the stage as a young Moroccan girl came shimmying out in my outfit. She was a hot little dancer and really showed off that fringe to full advantage. My services were, it seemed, no longer required, replaced by someone born and raised with the dance, so I retrieved the sweaty dress and left a little dejected.

Among the entertainers there was always talk of age. One Greek stripper was now 40 and many gossiped that she was too old, though she still looked fine to me. I was now thirty-seven and starting to see a few crow's feet (definitely laugh lines) at the corners of my eyes.

Just at that time came another call from Artur in Lisbon, profusely apologizing because the Dubai contract had been canceled, precisely on the basis of my age. The director of the Dubai hotel had liked my photos, yes, but later when a copy of my passport was sent with the final paperwork, they saw my birthdate and did not trust that the photos were current. I thought perhaps they also figured that younger girls were easier to control, but the rejection cut sharply. Much later Artur reported that the girl they did send for the job called every day crying that the authorities had taken her passport and kept her locked in her hotel room, so he was glad I had not gone. Disappointing as it was, I also was glad I did not end up in that dismal circumstance. Those guardian angels were on duty, as usual.

Before meeting Robert in Italy, I returned to Lisbon to box up my belongings for shipment to the U.S. and say good-byes to these great friends. Over the ensuing years we have kept in touch and visited back and forth on many occasions. Artur told me he could count on one hand the number of VIP, Very Important People, who had changed his life, and that I was one. "Because of your joy, your philosophy, your beauty." He wrote in a birthday card: "To drive you need a

'Driving License' and to LIVE you should have a 'LIVING LICENSE'!!! To me you gave a 'Living License' with your example, your smile, your art, your sweetness, your dreams! So such a teacher...should live forever...and you will, in our hearts! Thank you for being...you! Much Love, Artur."

I was moved to tears and told him he made my whole life suddenly make sense. At the end of 1984, these dear people were happy for me and so encouraging as they put me on a plane to Rome to begin a new chapter.

Athens, Greece 1984. Pro Photo Shoot,
Hand-sewn Costume

Athens, Greece 1984. Pro Photo Shoot, Red/Gold
Egyptian Dress

San Rafael, CA 1984. Home from Greece for Reunion,
Photo by Mom

Oakland, CA 1985. Entertaining Robert's friends,
Hand-sewn Costume

Italian Connection

"Closing my eyes to connect to my roots, I sense the wisdom of my ancestors and my grandmother smiles."
The Gossamer Path

Italy was exciting and "Roberto" a fine guide, knowing where to go and what to see. It was fun to meet his cousins who lived in the rural outskirts of Florence and kept little birds in cages all around the yard, which were served up at the raucous family meals (yes, they ate those cute little songbirds). The wine and grappa flowed freely. With my accumulation of French, Spanish, and Portuguese (and school Latin), I understood much of the conversation, and universal sign language filled in the rest. One female cousin took me aside to say, with the appropriate geometrical hand gestures, she was not so sure that Roberto and I went together well as I was so *rotonda* and he was such *un uomo quadrato,* a square man. *She* was so astute.

I was appropriately awed by my first glimpse of the wondrous city's art and architecture of the Uffizi and Pitti Palaces, the sculptures of Michelangelo, Brunelleschi's Duomo, the bronze doors and mosaic ceiling of the Baptistry, the miraculously preserved frescoes inside the many churches. I was transported by the tiled roof views and the bridges across the Arno, one still housing gold sellers' stalls. There Robert bought me a woven tri-color gold bracelet, but added the confusingly joyless message, "Don't get too used to it."

Some of my father's ancestors were from Sestri Levante on the Ligurian Riviera. We checked into a hotel there and the hotel clerk knew my family name. He called someone then and there, and soon an elegant lady came to meet us. Carniglia had been her maiden name, but she was now married with two young children living in a neighboring town. We were invited to their large, modern luxury apartment for dinner and shown around the fishing village and ancestral home the next day. How exciting to be on the exact beach where my paternal relatives had lived and worked!

Sestri is located on a small peninsula formed by a bay on one side with the Mediterranean Sea to the East. Some members of the family had immigrated from there to San Francisco as builders and fishermen before 1900 (they remembered the 1906 earthquake). From a gallery of sepia photos on the wall of a contemporary restaurant, times looked tough during turn-of-the-century in Sestri. Women appeared to be washing clothes in ditches along muddy dirt streets. The second evening there we joined my newfound family at their "country home" for a patio meal prepared in their private pizza oven. They were prospering in the current real estate boom and seemed to be living an ideal life in the 1984 version of the region.

Homeward Bound

"Traveling makes you realize what an immeasurably nice place much of America could be if only people possessed the same instinct for preservation as they do in Europe... Instead they just...build more parking lots and Pizza Huts."
Bill Bryson

Coming back to California to live in Robert's family home in Oakland meant such a big adjustment for me. I dove into the Bay Area belly dance scene and found occasional work at a Jack London Square Greek nightclub in Oakland and a few San Francisco restaurants. But Robert said staunchly that he "would not be a stage door Johnny" and did not consider dancing a real job. There was a large annual belly dance festival held at the Oakland Scottish Rite Temple, in its fourth year, where I signed up to dance. A reporter snapped my picture, which appeared in the Oakland Tribune, making me the poster child of the event.

No one knew who I was or where I had come from, but I gradually made a few dance friends, taking workshops from other teachers. One of them had a group called Natica Angilly's Poetic Dance Theater Company. When we met, she said, "You look poetic" and invited me to join. I immediately brought to her dancers a new level of professionalism with costuming and make-up. I put false eyelashes on them for the first time for a TV shoot.

Sidebar: false eyelashes are a tricky business. I had learned to wait until the *professional* glue was tacky, but not too dry. It is also helpful to angle the lash slightly upward and try not to follow the exact eye shape but leave space at the outer corners to "open up the eye." Eventually over the next few years I traveled with the company — dancing choreographies set to poetry — to Taiwan, Italy, Hungary, Las Vegas, Florida, and L.A. Ironically, in a small cafeteria-like venue in our guide's small Hungarian town, I asked Natica if she wanted us to wear the eyelashes. She rebuked me with, "If the San Francisco Opera came to this town, would they perform without full make-up?" I was tickled that she so completely adopted the aesthetic I had introduced when we first met.

I did try to fit in with Robert's business, duck-hunting, and baseball fan friends. It was a bit of a culture shock coming back into mainstream America after having been away for fifteen years of "fringe" adventures beginning in Montreal. Robert suggested that since I was good at sewing, I could become a seamstress, or, being a practiced wayfarer, I might become a travel agent. I recoiled from both of these "constructive" ideas, knowing that I was already so much more an artist than a humble-sounding seamstress and that I could not survive the confines of an office job, even if it included occasional traveling perks.

I still needed to develop a sustainable art form but realized it could no longer be based solely on dance. The few American venues for belly dancers paid appallingly little, and there were plenty of girls vying for the sparse regular gigs.

My family accepted Robert as one of their own. My mother was thrilled that he had brought me back from my wanderings, and my brother and sister both seemed to resonate with his style of humor much more than I could. He and his brother were carrying on their deceased father's business as developers and builders of office and warehouse spaces.

216

Whenever a building was completed, there was an "opening ceremony" which we all proudly attended.

I did realize that as a good Italian, Robert would want progeny, so I offered to have my tubal ligation reversed as a "young" and healthy woman of thirty-eight. He appreciated the magnitude of that suggestion but luckily it never came to pass, as I would never be able to conform to the old school model of a wife that befit his expectations.

Kismet

"Every single thing that has ever happened in your life is preparing you for a moment that is yet to come."
Mark Nepo

It soon became apparent that Robert and I had too little in common after an increasingly difficult year filled with misunderstandings. He apparently read my outgoing correspondence to friends across the globe and came up with the idea that I was no more than a "gold-digger" looking for a cushy life. He concluded that when I wrote to one girlfriend that I had finally found a man I did not have to help support. I moved across the bay into my mother's San Rafael home in Marin County.

At the time my paternal grandmother, living in a retirement community, was succumbing to colon cancer. Her eyesight was also failing, so on my regular visits I sorted through her mail and read it to her. There appeared a brochure for the Marin Civic Light Opera, announcing auditions for the upcoming show, *Kismet* (meaning fate), a sort of musical Arabian Nights set in ancient Baghdad. Though I had never seen the musical, I had grown up with its beautiful songs set to music by the Russian composer Alexander Borodin: "Stranger in Paradise," "Baubles, Bangles and Beads," "And This Is My Beloved." Assuming the show would require belly dancers, I went to the audition.

The first person to greet me in the green room was the main contender for the lead male role, Ken Rowland. He was dashing with the moustache and goatee he had grown for the part. Although already in his early fifties, Ken had the vitality of a boy. As he enthusiastically showed me an original score from the Alfred Drake Broadway production of the show, I could not help but notice the passion in his voice and sparkling eyes.

I "made the cut" into the show as a member of the general chorus and with a dance solo in the "Presentation of the Princesses" scene. Soon I was asked to be consultant to the choreographer and costumer to the harem girls. In addition, I was formally given the prop design job, working closely with the intriguing Ken as he built the beautiful sets.

We got along well, bouncing ideas back and forth, and always happy in each other's company. Though the cast was all volunteers from the community, the production team was paid, so I was surprised to garner small stipends for both giving private belly dance lessons to the choreographer and for my fun work as prop designer.

It became clear during rehearsals that Ken had a rich trained tenor voice and was a favorite with many regional theater companies. He played the lead in *South Pacific* (Emil Debeque), *My Fair Lady* (Professor Henry Higgins), and *Sound of Music* (Captain Von Trapp), and now The Poet Hajj in *Kismet*. He had studied opera and brought all his expertise to musical theater. I marveled over his stage presence, impeccable acting and singing. And I was enamored!

We were fifteen years minus one day apart, both artistic, individualistic Aquarians (him February 13, me February 14). During the rehearsal period I danced for Ken's birthday at a cast party given by the director. He seemed quite pleased, seeing me for the first time in full costume, displaying my talents and openly flirting with him.

It seemed he too was smitten. Soon, on our first date, over our twin plates of pasta *frutti di mare,* Ken divulged that what was most important to him in life was theater. Finally a kindred spirit! It was not a stretch for me to agree that performing and creating theatrical settings were also my passions. And theater was an opportunity for me to combine my many artistic chops I had developed over the years. One day he brought to my mother's house a portfolio of costume and set designs he had created for a local opera, and I was thoroughly impressed. My heart was all aflutter as we courted during the run of the show. I found myself singing "And This Is My Beloved" and telling myself had never before known what love truly was.

Reviewing my several past relationships, I had certainly learned what love was *not*! Many of those had been so unrealistic, based purely on sex, or in the most recent case, trying to reshape myself into an unsuitably square mold. Here was a person with whom I could truly share myself and my life — what every woman longs for and deserves.

And so it was that Ken eventually invited me to move into his craftsman home, a sort of stage set in itself. It was thrilling to be initiated into a new fulfilling career with a new exciting romantic partner, the leading man who could appreciate me for who I actually was. And I could continue with dancing as teacher, troupe director, performer and costume designer without intimidating him. We were completely supportive of each other's arts, so this seemed a less risky but more alive choice.

Ken had two grown sons, both with children, and he brought me to meet them at their homes in northern counties (Sonoma and Mendocino). As I got to know them, I became like an Auntie, enjoying their company and babysitting privileges, a plus for me since I would never have my own grandchildren.

Ken also proved to be a great mentor. I learned so much about theater, opera, period costumes, history, classical music, elocution, *backstage* drama, and much more from the illustrious Renaissance Man. We shared many adventures working as an artistic team for regional theater and opera companies, including Marin's famed annual Mountain Play production at the amphitheater atop Mt. Tamalpais.

I even went back to school at age 40 to ace all my classes in the drama department of our local College of Marin and eventually worked there. We traveled together to absorb London Theater, Italian Art, and Scottish Standing Stones, all quite differently than I had previously traveled. Ah, but those stories are fermenting for the next book!

It was truly *Kismet.*

San Rafael, CA 1986. Kenneth
Rowland as The Hajj in *Kismet*

Mill Valley, CA 1987. Dhyanis with the band "Sirocco" at
Cairo Cafe

Epilogue – The Goddess

"Who is she? She is your power, your Feminine source. Big Mama. The Goddess. The Great Mystery. The web-weaver. The life force. The first time, the twentieth time, you may not recognize her...But when she calls you will know you've been called. Then it is up to you to decide if you will answer." Lucy H. Pearce

All the while dance formed the core of my lifestyle — and still does — but took a new direction. With my theater contacts I began producing annual shows based on research into ancient matriarchal societies and their Goddess-oriented religions. I called it "The Living Goddess Dance Theater Production" and each year explored a different pantheon of goddesses from many cultures and many eras. I became an ordained Priestess of the Goddess Isis. One of my students was a psychotherapist and a member of the American Holistic Nurses Association. We put together weekend retreats for nurses, as well as Mother/Daughter, Sisters, and general Feminine Empowerment workshops.

I later remarried at the age of fifty-two to a wonderful man, John, who helped bring both a Masked Dance Company, Tuju Taksu (which means Aiming for the Divine Spirit which Manifests Through Art, and with whom I danced for ten years), and my own award-winning belly dance Troupe

Dhyanis to the Edinburgh Fringe Festival of the Arts in 1999 and 2000 consecutively.

This man has a son born with cerebral palsy, in a wheelchair, whom I helped raise from age nine when his mother gave him up to marry someone else who did not want her to keep her disabled son. We became an instant family. I opened a dance studio in the form of a Goddess Temple with a boutique for "Goddesswear" mostly made by me, and designed a line of beaded goods and batiks developed with a family in Bali.

After the dance studio closed in 2010, a decade before this writing, I studied Grief Coaching and have helped many clients through losses such as I experienced. The program at The Grief Coach Academy, put together by the brilliant and compassionate Aurora Winter opened my life to many new activities and areas of study, which evolve to this day.

So the adventure continues, and this book is intended to become the first of a trilogy with later books delving more into both theater experiences and the more practical and spiritual sides of the Goddess Path.

About the Author

While continuing to teach and perform the most ancient women's dance, Dhyanis has also served for seven years as a Hospice Volunteer. She is an officer at her branch of Toastmasters International and has enhanced her public speaking skills.

She is planning more workshops and is available for speaking engagements. One specialty has become "Releasing Grief Through Movement."

If you enjoyed this book, please leave a book review on Amazon.

Contact Dhyanis at **dhyanis@movingpastgrief.com**, or through either her dance website **www.dhyanis.com** or her grief relief website **www.movingpastgrief.com**.

Facebook Page: Dhyanis Carniglia

Made in the USA
Monee, IL
05 April 2021

63699552R00134